THE RAMBLERS' ASSOCIATION

LAKE DISTRICT WALKS WITH A POINT

THE RAMBLERS' ASSOCIATION

LAKE DISTRICT WALKS WITH A POINT

Colin Shelbourn

W. Foulsham & Co. Ltd.
London · New York · Toronto · Cape Town · Sydney

The Ramblers' Association
1-5 Wandsworth Rd,
London SW8 2LJ

W. Foulsham & Company Limited
Yeovil Road, Slough, Berkshire, SL1 4JH

Author's Acknowledgements
I am very grateful to the following for their assistance: Pam Grant and Lorna Shelbourn, for their help with the walks; Diane Ellwood, for her invaluable knowledge of Lakeland flora; and John Wyatt, for guidance and encouragement. Finally I would like to thank whoever is responsible for making 1985 one of the wettest Lake District summers on record . . .

Colin Shelbourn

ISBN 0-572-01355-8

Please note:
Although every effort has been made to ensure that the details given in this book are accurate, the author, the publishers and the Ramblers' Association cannot accept responsibility for any changes or alterations to the information since the research was carried out. Where public rights of way are concerned any obstacle or hindrance should be reported to the Ramblers' Association (see page 9).

Printed in Great Britain
at St. Edmundsbury Press,
Bury St. Edmunds.

Cover Photo: Dove Cottage, Grasmere
(Walk 6). Courtesy of The Dove Cottage Trust.

INFORMATION ABOUT THE RAMBLERS' ASSOCIATION

The Ramblers' Association is a registered charity with three main aims:

- to protect footpaths and other rights of way and increase access to open country.
- to defend outstanding landscapes.
- to encourage people to walk in the countryside.

It carries out these aims at a national level, through the employment of staff to run national campaigns, lobby MPs, etc. and generally organise the work of the Association, and at a local level through the activities of the voluntary workers in its Areas and Groups, who tackle problems on paths, both by reporting them to highway authorities and by carrying out practical work, such as stile building and waymaking. The Areas and Groups also have programmes of rambles and other events.

Since it was formed in 1935 the RA has grown steadily, and in 1985 membership topped 50,000 for the first time. The RA's branch structure has also developed, in particular through the formation of local Groups within Areas.

The threats to the countryside and its paths are growing, and so are our needs. You can help simply by becoming a member. There are plenty of opportunities for joining in the practical footpath and amenity work carried out by your local RA Group.

As a member you will be able to take advantage of the following benefits.

■ A **local group** to walk with (but go on your own if you prefer); most groups run social events too. ■ Free annual **Bed and Breakfast Guide** with more than 2,000 addresses where walkers are welcome. ■ **Rucksack**, the RA's own magazine, plus your own area news, four times a year. ■ Use of our 1:50,000 Ordnance Survey **map library**. ■ **Discounts** in more than 100 outdoor equipment shops. ■ **Special offers on publications**; a discount subscription to **The Great Outdoors** magazine. ■ Access to our national service of **expert advice and information**.

PROTECTING THE FOOTPATH HERITAGE

INTRODUCTION

The information given below is about the law relating to public rights of way in England and Wales.

Public paths are highways in law. They have the same legal protection in principle as metalled carriageways, the difference being that paths are dedicated to use by limited classes of traffic, i.e. walkers on footpaths; and walkers, riders and cyclists on bridleways.

An old legal maxim says that once a highway always a highway. This means that a public path can only be closed by statutory procedure. It does not cease to be a right of way simply because it is unused or little used.

HOW YOU CAN HELP

Paths are part of our heritage and need our protection. Every time you walk along a path you help to keep it open. By varying routes to include little known paths and by reporting any difficulties you meet you can make every step count in the struggle to preserve our country walks.

Reporting difficulties. Write to the appropriate local authority (see below) and tell the RA. Give location (six figure grid reference) and nature of problem, path number and name of owner or tenant (if known). RA national office will supply you with obstruction report forms ready for use.

Obstructions. An obstruction is anything which hinders your free passage along the path, e.g. a barbed wire fence where there should be a gap or stile. County councils have a statutory duty to keep public paths open for public use and enjoyment.

Ploughing. It is illegal to plough a path along a field boundary. The farmer is required to leave room between the hedge or fence and the cultivated area for the path. Paths going across fields may be ploughed, provided that the farmer restores the path within two weeks of ploughing. Report infringements to county or district councils.

Bridges and overgrowth. A missing bridge or overgrowth on the surface of the path are within the highway authority's maintenance responsibilities. The highway authorities are the county councils but some district councils have taken over maintenance from the counties. Overgrowth from the sides of the path should be dealt with by the owner or tenant of the land. The highway authority has power to act if he does not.

Misleading notices, i.e. any signs which by false or misleading information may deter people from using a public path, are an offence on paths shown on the definitive map. Report to highway authority.

Bulls. No bull over the age of ten months is allowed to be at large on its own in a field crossed by a public path, and no bull of a recognised dairy breed (Ayrshire, British Friesian, British Holstein, Dairy Shorthorn, Guernsey, Jersey and Kerry) is allowed in such a field under any circumstances. It is not a specific offence for beef and cross breed bulls to be at large in fields crossed by public paths if they are accompanied by cows or heifers, but if the bull endangers public safety an offence may be committed under section 3 of the Health and Safety at Work Act 1974. Report any problems to the police.

PRACTICAL WORK

Increasingly, branches of the RA and local footpath and amenity societies are undertaking practical work to improve the condition of the paths.

This takes two main forms: path clearance and waymarking. Waymarking is carried out by painting arrows at points along the path where the route is unclear.

FURTHER READING

A brief exposition of the law in England and Wales is contained in a leaflet published by the RA, *Right of Way*. The RA also publishes, in conjunction with the Open Spaces Society, *Rights of Way: a Guide to Law and Practice*, a comprehensive 368-page book which includes the text of the relevant legislation. The RA also sells *Footpaths: a practical handbook* published by the British Trust for Conservation Volunteers, which is a most comprehensive guide to practical work.

CONTENTS

Symbol	Meaning	Symbol	Meaning
	Route and direction of walk	PH	Public house
A385	A Road		Settlement
B3212	B Road		Building
	All other roads and tracks		Church
	Footpath		Bridge
	Railway		Weir
	Canal		Quarry
P	Parking		Triangulation pillar
	Viewpoint		Woodland
	Golf course		Lake
			Tumulus
			Cairn

The maps

The sketch maps in this book are meant to be used in conjunction with the Ordnance Survey map mentioned at the beginning of each walk. Symbols on the maps have been simplified and are meant to give rough guidance to the location of symbols on the Ordnance Survey map.

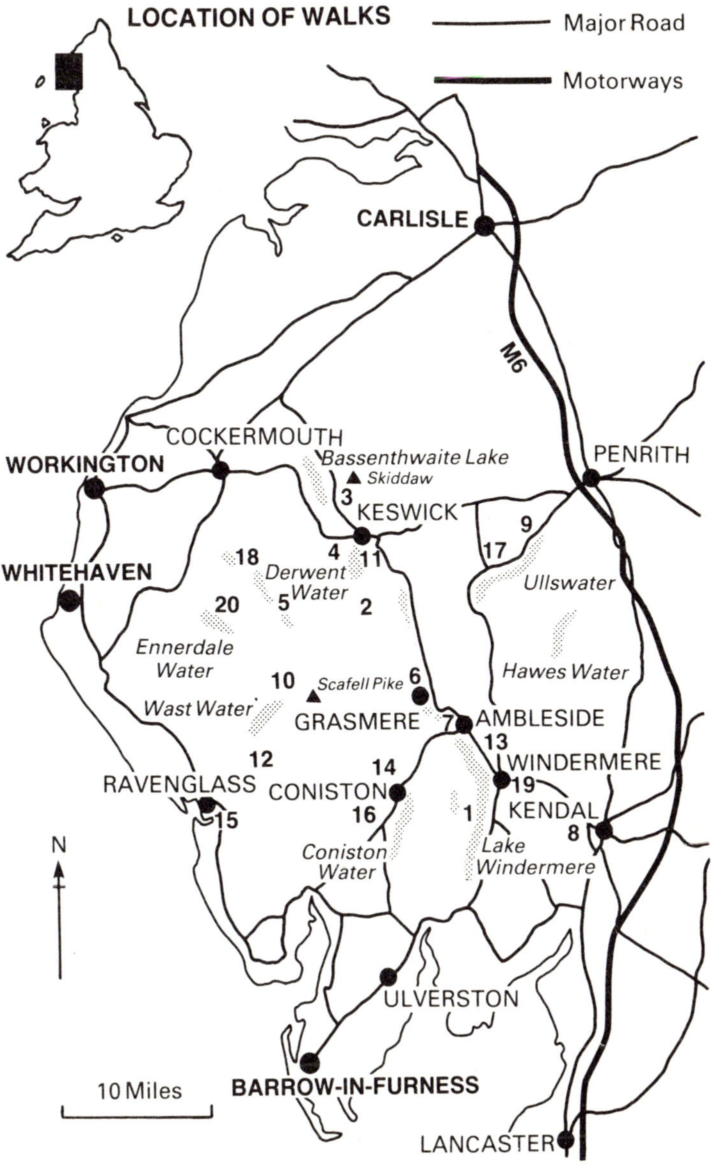

LOCATION OF WALKS
Major Road
Motorways
CARLISLE
M6
COCKERMOUTH
WORKINGTON
Bassenthwaite Lake
Skiddaw
PENRITH
3
KESWICK
9
17
4
11
18
WHITEHAVEN
Derwent
Water
5
2
Ullswater
20
Ennerdale
Water
Hawes Water
10
Scafell Pike
6
Wast Water
GRASMERE
7
AMBLESIDE
13
12
WINDERMERE
14
19
RAVENGLASS
CONISTON
KENDAL
16
1
15
8
N
Coniston
Water
Lake
Windermere
ULVERSTON
10 Miles
BARROW-IN-FURNESS
LANCASTER

WALK 1
LITERARY
BEATRIX POTTER AND HILL TOP

(Cockshott Point – Far Sawrey)

Beatrix Potter's house, Hill Top, is the most popular of all Lakeland's literary homes, receiving more visitors each year than any of the Wordsworth properties.

MAPS:	O/S 1:25,000 Outdoor Leisure Series, 'The English Lakes' , S-E sheet.
DISTANCE:	6 miles.
ROUGH GUIDE TO TIME TAKEN:	3–3½ hours.
TERRAIN:	A steep climb up Claife with some potentially muddy footpaths. Thereafter level walking along footpaths and bridleways.
FOOD AND DRINK:	Tower Bank Arms, Near Sawrey.
TRANSPORT:	Glebe Road car park, Bowness. (Grid reference: 402966).
START AND FINISH:	Bowness Bay National Park Information Centre, Bowness.
ADDITIONAL NOTES:	Hill Top, Near Sawrey, Hawkshead. (Tel: Hawkshead 269).

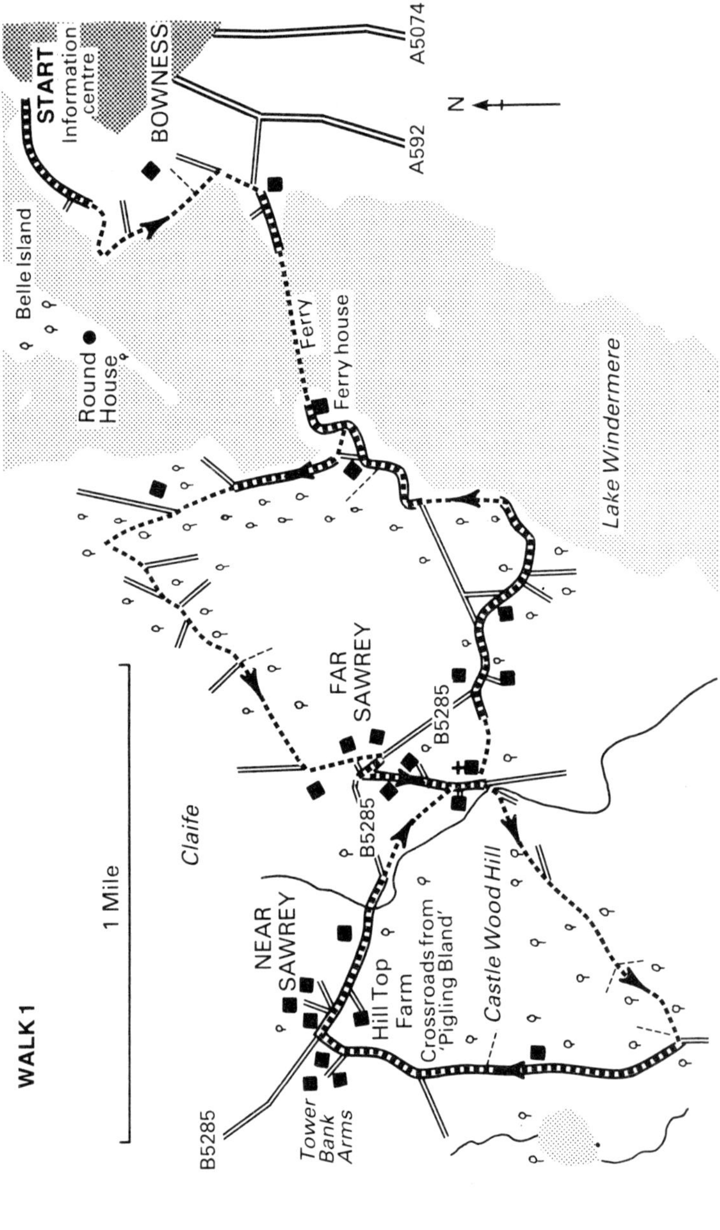
WALK 1
START
Information centre
BOWNESS
A5074
A592
N
Belle Island
Round House
Ferry
Ferry house
Lake Windermere
FAR SAWREY
B5285
B5285
Claife
1 Mile
NEAR SAWREY
Hill Top Farm
Crossroads from 'Pigling Bland'
Castle Wood Hill
B5285
Tower Bank Arms

Open: Easter to end of October. Daily except Friday:
Mon – Sat 10.00–5.30
Sunday 2.00–5.30 (Last admission 5.00)

Park at Glebe Road car park, behind the Bowness Bay National Park information centre. Leave the car park by the main entrance and turn left down Glebe road, past the information centre and Shepherd's boat yards. (At the height of summer, this part of the walk can be hazardous with tourists and traffic hurtling in all directions. Get up early and do it before the crowds are about.) Continue past the boat chandlers on your right until you come to a wooded park directly in front of you, marked National Trust – Cockshott Point. Go through the iron gate and follow the footpath.

On your right you will see Windermere's only inhabited island, Belle Isle, with its circular house. The island used to be called Long Holme and the house was built in 1774 by Thomas English. It is said to be the only completely circular house in the country. In 1781, the island was bought by Isabella Curwen and the island renamed after her. It remains in the Curwen family to this day. During the summer the Bowness Bay Boating Company run regular launches to the island and there are guided tours of the house as well as a nature trail around the island itself. A good place for a summer picnic.

Continue through Cockshott Point and along the lake shore to an iron gate. Go through and turn right along the track, which brings you into the car park and public launch site. Go straight through, turn right at the road and follow it to the ferry. Windermere's ferry runs all year round (including Sundays) and crosses the lake at its narrowest point (700 yards). It leaves the Bowness side every twenty minutes. Long queues of traffic can build up in summer but foot passengers generally have no problem getting across and it is very cheap.

As you cross you get a good view of the northern half of the lake and another look at Belle Isle. There has been a ferry on this spot for at least 500 years. The old ferries were rowed across; peer over the side and you'll see that the modern ferry pulls itself across via two steel cables. Once on the far shore, follow the road past Ferry House, the large grey building on your left. Once a hotel, it now houses the Freshwater Biological Association. Just past the building, look for a footpath sign on your right. The path follows the wooded shoreline to a tarmac road. Turn right and follow the road into the National Trust's Claife Estate.

At the cattle grid, take the permitted path on your left and begin to climb up through the woods. You start to get good views downhill to the lake. The path crosses several small streams and climbs steadily uphill through mature mixed woodland. If doing this walk in springtime, listen out for green woodpeckers.

The path reaches a 'T junction'. Turn left and continue walking uphill through the trees. At the five-bar gate at the top of the hill, the path continues between two stone walls, waymarked 'To Hawkshead and Sawrey'. (By now the sound of power boats and lake activity is fading and it is very peaceful – only the sounds of sheep and birdlife.) The path continues beyond another five-bar gate to a crossroads, with three gates and waymarking. You should continue to follow the route marked 'Bridleway to Sawrey', through the middle gate, and walking through rich pasture land. Once over the brow of the hill there are superb views across the geologically softer sedimentary rocks of Grizedale Forest to the peak of Consion Old Man, rising sharply above the forest plateau. To the right is Wetherlam.

The track winds downhill to Far Sawrey. As you descend, Near Sawrey and Hill Top (on your left) can be seen as a cluster of houses a few fields away. Still going downhill, follow the stony track through the next five-bar gate and on to a narrow lane. At the main Hawkshead road, turn right towards the Sawrey Hotel, then immediately left down the road to Sawrey church (opposite the hotel entrance). Notice the traditional method of walling around Hawkshead – large stone slates placed on end rather than drystone walls.

The road winds past a farmstead to St. Peter's Church. Immediately after the group of cottages, look out for a footpath sign on your right. Go through the kissing-gate (next to a farm gate). The path bears away to the right of a cart track and you arrive at a stile, to the left of another gate. Go over and continue round the contour of the hill. This rough land at the edge of the meadow has an abundance of wild flowers. At the next five-bar gate, look out for a stile and gate (not signed). Go over the stile to your right, *not* through the gate, and along the track. At the top of the rise another stile leads into woods. Note the deer fence and high gate to your left. Follow the track, skirting the deer fence for about ¼ mile, reaching the road via two stiles. Turn right and follow the road.

Beatrix Potter's books were often illustrated with scenes from around Sawrey and Hawkshead, all of which were painted on site rather than from memory. As you follow this lane, you can see the Langdales and Esthwaite Water on your left – a similar view can be found in *The Tale of Jeremy Fisher.* Shortly you will arrive at a road junction, illustrated in *The Tale of Pigling Bland*, with only minor changes visible from the original painting.

At the junction, go right into Near Sawrey, then keep right again at the next fork and turn right again when you reach the main Hawkshead road.

Beatrix Potter was born in London in 1865 and spent holidays in the Lake District as a child, her family connected with the Lancashire cotton trade. She began writing and illustrating her books at the encouragement of Canon Rawnsley, a family friend. Her first book, *Peter Rabbit*, was published in 1895. She bought Hill Top Farm in 1905, though never actually lived there, using it as a sort of holiday home. With the income from her books, she began to buy property. Following her marriage to her solicitor, William Heelis, in 1913, she devoted herself to farming and the countryside.

Beatrix Potter died in 1943, leaving a total of 15 farms and 4,000 acres to the National Trust.

The Trust owns Hill Top and it is one of the most visited houses in the country. It contains her furniture and china, though her fine, original illustrations are no longer on display.

The houses in the village will be familiar to readers of *The Pie and the Patty Pan*, *Jeremy Fisher* and *Tom Kitten*. The Tower Bank Arms pub (also owned by the N.T.) features in *Jemima Puddleduck*, along with Hill Top itself.

From Hill Top, turn right and continue along the road, over the brow of the hill to a clearly signed footpath on the right. Through a kissing-gate and over a footbridge, the path follows a field boundary and stream on your left. After the second footbridge, the path crosses a meadow to another kissing-gate.

You are now about to cross the line of an earlier section of the walk. Turn right to pass the church and find a footpath sign on your left. Go through the kissing-gate and up to the top of the field, where you will find another kissing-gate. The path leads you down to the Hawkshead road (again!). Turn right and follow road to a junction by a sharp bend, giving you a good view over the lake.

Turn right, past some pleasant, large houses. At the next fork, keep right and continue downhill. At Bryers Cottage, turn left and continue down lane to lakeshore. There is private land to either side of the track. Go through the old gate pillars and follow the tree-lined track along the shoreline. It emerges about half-a-mile from the ferry landing. Follow the road back to the ferry and reverse route back to Bowness Bay.

WALK 2
LITERARY
WATENDLATH AND DOCK TARN

(Rosthwaite – Hazel Bank – Watendlath – Stonethwaite)

Watendlath is a small, attractive hamlet standing beside a tarn, high above the Borrowdale Valley. It was the setting for Sir Hugh Walpole's novel, *Judith Paris*, and her fictional home is now marked by a plaque.

MAPS:	O/S 1:25,000 Outdoor Leisure Series, 'The English Lakes' , N-W sheet.
DISTANCE:	$4\frac{1}{2}$ miles.
ROUGH GUIDE TO TIME TAKEN:	4 hours.
TERRAIN:	Steep in places with muddy and boggy patches.
FOOD AND DRINK:	Public bar at Scafell Hotel (Rosthwaite ice cream also highly recommended.)
TRANSPORT:	Car park down lane opposite Rosthwaite Post Office (Grid reference: 257148).
START AND FINISH:	Rosthwaite.

WALK 2

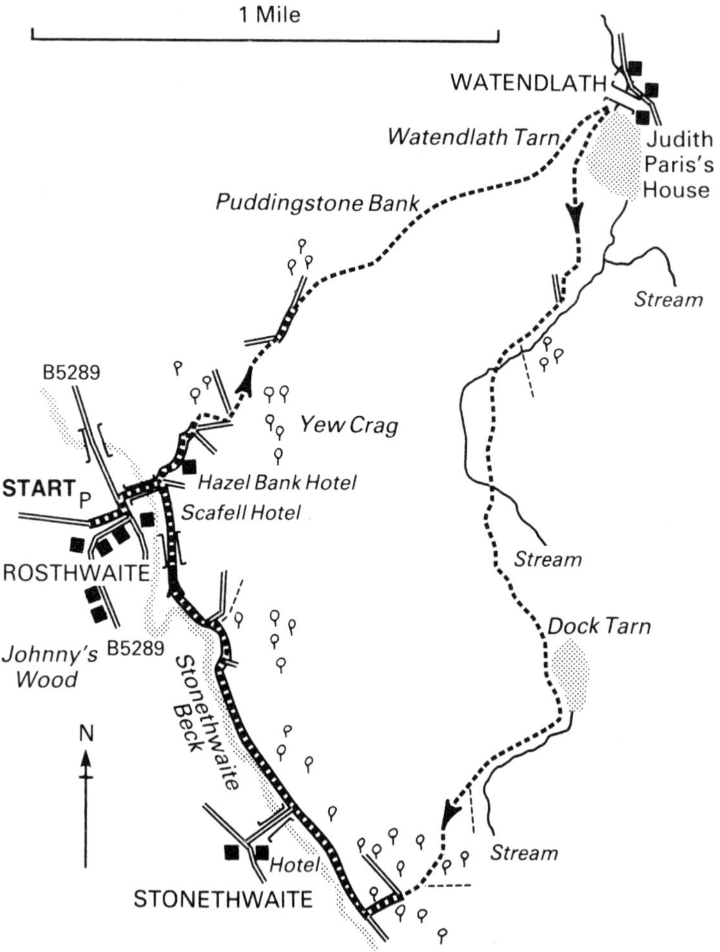
1 Mile
WATENDLATH
Watendlath Tarn
Judith Paris's House
Puddingstone Bank
Stream
B5289
Yew Crag
START
P
Hazel Bank Hotel
Scafell Hotel
ROSTHWAITE
Stream
Dock Tarn
Johnny's Wood
B5289
Stonethwaite Beck
N
Stream
Hotel
STONETHWAITE

Park at the car park 100 yards down the lane opposite Rosthwaite Post Office. Walk back along the lane to the Post Office and turn left along the main road. After 10 yards on the right is a roadway, marked Hazel Bank Hotel, which leads over Stonethwaite Beck. Follow this road over the bridge and you come to a junction. Turn left at Hazel Bank on to a footpath and along some solid slabs of stone. Once across a beck, via a concrete ramp, you turn right through a farm gate and on to a bridleway climbing gently uphill. The fellside opens up with a gill on your right. Shortly you come to a junction, one path forking sharp left to follow a fence, the other continuing gradually uphill. Take the latter, passing alongside rowan and larch trees.

After 200 yards, the path winds steeply up to a well-marked footpath and you reach a gap in the wall. Turn left and follow the well-defined footpath across the fell-side, heading towards a small conifer wood. The small, steep crag which can be seen on your right is Yew Crag. On reaching the next stone wall, the footpath flattens out and there is an excellent view across the valley of Rosthwaite, Borrowdale and Johnny's Wood.

Cross a footbridge and pass under a Scots Pine, with a wall on your left. Off to the left, you can see a conifer wood, made up of a number of interesting species. A footpath left at this point is marked 'Keswick and Bowder Stone', but you should ignore this path and continue uphill, past a group of Scots Pine on your left. The path keeps to the left of a deep gorge until it crosses the gill via a footbridge and flattens out once again. A little farther, away from the treeline, turn round at the broken wall for fine views back over Borrowdale.

Continue uphill and the path flattens out above Puddingstone Bank, crossing a wall via a gate and stile. Note the hog hole in the wall on your right. The path runs along a damp, marshy area to your right, often rich in common marsh orchid and bog asphodil. Now comes the descent to Watendlath, keeping to a well-marked foot-

Ridge behind. A steep descent down a boulder-strewn path brings you to a gate, immediately before the tarn.

As you descend, look across the tarn for a white house on the far right, beside the farm. This was the fictional home of Judith Paris, the tempestuous heroine of the second of Hugh Walpole's 'Herries Chronicles'. Written in the early 1930's, the novels (*Rogue Herries, Judith Paris, The Fortress* and *Vanessa*) were each set in the Lake District. In the same way that Thomas Hardy brought to life the countryside of Wessex, Walpole peopled the landscape around Keswick and Borrowdale with the wild, passionate descendants of old Rogue Herries.

Turn left through a gate. The tarn is well-stocked with trout and you will notice the outlet has a barrier across it to prevent them from escaping. Cross over a small pack-horse bridge, turning right to the buildings. The house on the left sells teas and scones. Farther on, through the farmyard, is Fold Head farmhouse. Now a bed and breakfast, the farmhouse has a slate plaque which reads 'Judith Paris's Home'.

It is only in the last few years that mains electricity has come to Watendlath. The inhabitants lit up a Christmas Tree in the car park to celebrate. In 1984 a telephone cable was first laid, buried alongside the footpath you have just followed. Watendlath can be reached by car, but not in summer as the road gets clogged with cars, none of the drivers having time for the view.

To continue to Dock Tarn, retrace your steps over the packhorse bridge, through a gate on the lakeshore and follow the signed path to Dock Tarn. This takes you along the lakeshore for 100 yards and brings you to a pair of gates. Go through the right-hand gate (signed "Path"), by a pollarded ash, and follow a broad track across enclosed land, leaving the tarn behind on the left. More pollarded trees can be seen along this route. Eventually you reach a gate and a traditional stone stile by a beck. The footpath follows the beck for a little while, then bends to the right by an arrowed sign. A grassy path is followed to another beck and yet another arrow pointing to the right, just past a distinctive wall corner. The footpath now heads uphill, beside the beck, amongst large, scattered rocks and small, birch-topped crags.

Eventually, you reach a locked gate in a stone wall. Cross by the ladderstile alongside. The Right of Way follows the wall to the left, once across the stile, but a more obvious footpath goes straight ahead, keeping to the wall and then a fence on your right side, until it can be seen to bear off left, away from the wall. 50 yards onwards, a sloping-topped boulder, about three feet high, marks our path. It bears left across rough bracken and heather. This area can get very boggy. Bog myrtle is found in abundance – the leaves should be smelled to be fully appreciated.

Head towards an obvious wall between two broad crags; after the kissing gate, the route heads up a steep, eroded path beyond. The ground flattens out by a 10 feet high flake of rock to the right of the path. Dock Tarn is now only 300 yards away and a well-cairned path leads to it. The footpath is well marked along the west side of the tarn (the side with the small trees, if you've forgotten your compass) until it goes off to the right, beside the outlet beck, following more cairns. Before going downhill, pause for the view – looking out towards Glaramara in front of you, and Sour Milk Gill with Gillercombe above. Honister Quarry can be seen farther to the right, rising up to Dales Head.

The footpath now follows a deepening ravine after several prominent cairns and is well marked, even though rocky. Where the path leaves the gill, it crosses a stretch of open grass amongst the bracken and down to a stile over a stone wall. Langstrath opens up before you (looking south) with Greenup Gill hidden behind Eagle and Sergeant Crag. The path drops steeply through a ruined wall, leaving the deep gorge on the left and passing by the ruins of two small buildings. (Reader quiz: What was the narrow opening in the bottom of the wall of the lower building?). From here you can see Greenup hill and Stonethwaite camp site, with Seatoller off to the right.

The path from here becomes much steeper and care should be taken. The descent is through an oak wood. Near the bottom of the wood the footpath rejoins Willygrass Gill, below waterfalls. Climb the stile and continue down to the open valley bottom. Just prior to leaving the wood, note the strange curved wall standing alone on your left. You meet up with a walled track, just clear of the woods; turn right, through a gate, and follow round past a sheepfold on your right. You next reach a gate and a decision is called for; a turn left here will take you over the bridge to Stonethwaite. However, a more interesting way back to Rosthwaite is via the original road, known as Back o' Beck. Toss a coin and then turn right. This leads you past the holly trees and a group of giant boulders. At the next pair of gates, take the lower one. At the next pair, take the left hand gate and follow the path back to Rosthwaite Bridge.

WALK 3
LITERARY
ST. BEGA'S CHURCH AND MIREHOUSE

(Dodd Wood – St. Bega's Church – Mirehouse)

This is an easy, low-level walk beside the shores of Bassenthwaite Lake to Mirehouse, a lovely English Manor House with many notable literary and historical connections. The family home of the Speddings, it has only recently opened to the public and remains unspoilt and uncrowded.

MAPS:	O/S 1:25,000 Outdoor Leisure Series, 'The English Lakes' , N-W sheet.
DISTANCE:	3 miles.
ROUGH GUIDE TO TIME TAKEN:	$1\frac{1}{2}$–2 hours (allow an additional 45 minutes to visit Mirehouse).
TERRAIN:	A gentle climb through Dodd Wood, thereafter level footpaths, possibly wet and muddy in places across fields.
FOOD AND DRINK:	The Old Sawmill, Dodd Wood car park.
TRANSPORT:	Dodd Wood car park, Mirehouse (Grid reference: 235282).
START AND FINISH:	Dodd Wood car park.

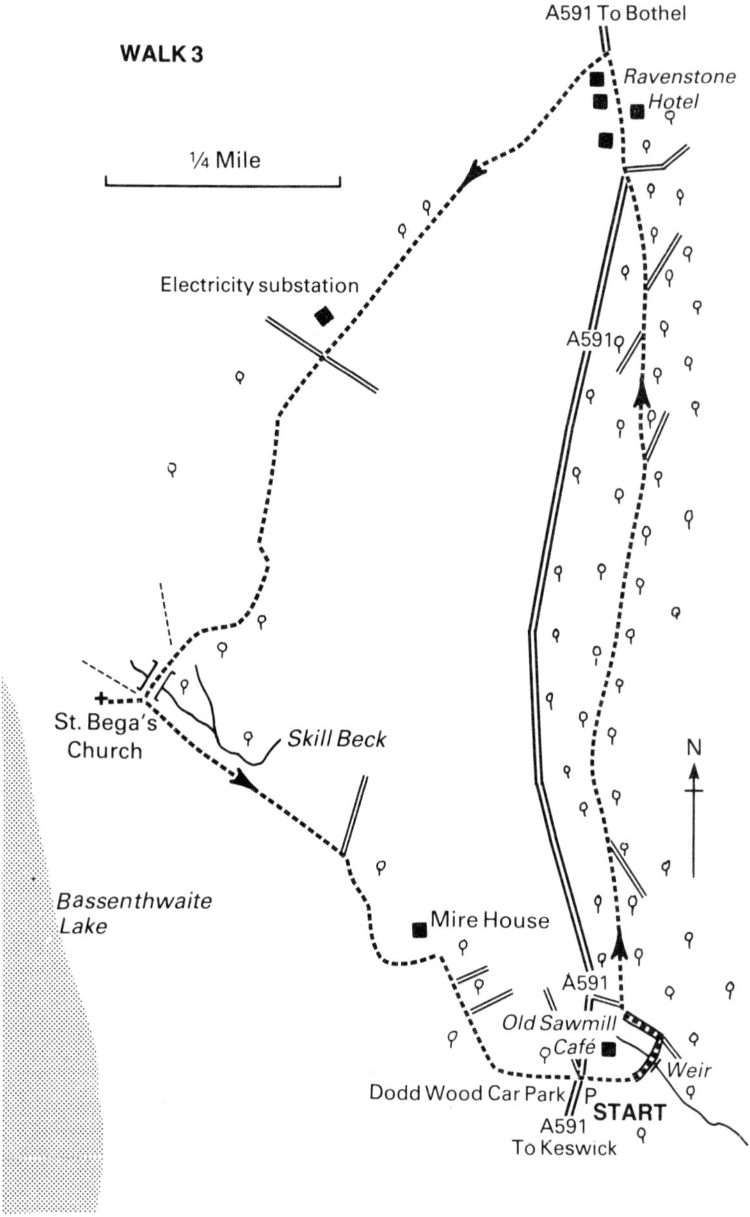

WALK 3
¼ Mile
A591 To Bothel
Ravenstone
Hotel
Electricity substation
A591
St. Bega's
Church
Skill Beck
Bassenthwaite
Lake
N
Mire House
A591
Old Sawmill
Café
Weir
Dodd Wood Car Park
P
START
A591
To Keswick

ADDITIONAL NOTES:	Mirehouse is open to the public from April to October on Wednesdays, Sundays and Bank Holiday Mondays, 2.00 to 5.00. Telephone Keswick (0596) 72287.

Park at Dodd Wood car park, 4 miles north of Keswick on the A591, on the eastern shores of Bassenthwaite Lake. Walk back through the car park to the Old Sawmill tea rooms. (This was the original mill building, built about 1880. The old water-powered saw remains and there are interesting displays of old forest tools inside. The teas are pretty good too.) Behind the Old Sawmill, cross Skill Beck via the footbridge and climb up to the tarmac forestry road. Turn left and head back towards the A591 for about 50 yards before turning off to your right. This is not a public right of way but is clear and easy to follow. The path climbs into the conifers, running roughly parallel with the main road. This whole area belongs to the Mirehouse estate and is leased to the Forestry Commission. The path levels off at a rock face. A turn right here would take you to the top of the Dodd, an excellent viewpoint overlooking Bassenthwaite Lake. However, you should go left, continuing around the flanks of the hill and coming into view of the lake.

A local joke is that there is only one lake in the Lake District, and that is Bassenthwaite. The rest are all 'meres' or 'waters'.

The path winds round the side of the hill, past a young sitka spruce plantation which will, in a few years, obscure the view. The path narrows and crosses a small beck before beginning to descend again. Ahead is a good view of Binsey. Ignore the path coming in from the left and, as you approach the main road, the path forks. Go right, over a pair of stiles and down to the road beside the Ravenstone Hotel.

path over fairly flat ground until the tarn and valley come into view immediately below you, with Ullscarf

Turn right along the road (taking great care), passing in front of the hotel. Just past the white bungalow on your left, cross the road and look for a sign (marked 'Public Footpath') and a series of steps. Take this path, through a farm gate and into fields. Straight across the first field and through a kissing-gate. The path disappears in the next field, but following the peculiar curved terrace of land will bring you to a group of trees, where you should turn left towards a stile in a wire fence. Cross the stile and the path once more becomes obvious, leading you through a line of trees and across two more fields to emerge on to a minor road beside an electricity substation. On the opposite side of the road is a farm gate, marked 'Car Park, St. Bega's Church'. Cross the stile alongside and follow the track through the fields to the church.

St. Bega's is one of the most romantically situated churches in the Lake District, on the shore of Bassenthwaite Lake, over $\frac{1}{2}$-a-mile from the road and farm from any settlement. The present church is Norman in origin but its circular churchyard and its situation beside the stream suggest to some that it may have had pagan origins. St. Bega, tradition has it, was an Irish noble-lady who founded a Benedictine nunnery on the west coast of Cumbria, around 650 A.D. The nunnery later gave its name to the nearby village – St. Bees. Services are still held at St. Bega's – the stone cross just outside the churchyard is sometimes used for open-air services. Today, worshippers have to walk across the fields but at one time, when Bassenthwaite Lake was the major highway, they would have arrived by boat. Alfred Lord Tennyson made use of the setting in his epic poem' 'Morte d'Arthur'; St. Bega's is the "chapel in the fields" where the dying King Arthur was carried by Sir Bedivere before he was borne away across the "great water".

Return to the track, but do not cross the stream. Instead, turn right, walking alongside the magnificent oaks towards Mirehouse. The view of the house across open parkland, with the Dodd rising in the background, is most impressive. You will cross a footbridge and come to a farm gate. Go through the stile alongside and along a hedge-lined path to the house. When you come to the junction in the paths, go right, following the path in front of the house.

Mirehouse is a splendid example of an English Manor House. The original, central, part of the house was built by the 8th Earl of Derby as a hunting lodge, in 1666. It was later sold to his agent Roger Gregg and passed through their family until 1802, when it was left to John Spedding of Armathwaite Hall. It has remained in the Spedding family ever since and has accumulated a unique record of the Speddings and their contemporaries. John Spedding spent six years in the same classroom as Wordsworth, at Hawkshead Grammar School, and his youngest son, James, was a close friend of Tennyson and Thomas Carlyle. Tennyson stayed at the house whilst writing his version of the Arthurian legend and Carlyle described Mirehouse as "beautiful and so were the ways of it . . . not to speak of Skiddaw and the finest mountains on Earth". Today the promotion of Mirehouse is deliberately low-key. The downstairs rooms are opened up on only two afternoons a week but are full of literary and historical interest, including papers and letters from the Lake poets.

Carry on past the house and you will come to a group of fine larch trees. Look out for a massive tree stump – the original tree was planted in 1829 (try counting the rings!). The route you are following is the only public right of way through the grounds, but there is a forest trail, available from the Old Sawmill. An admission fee is payable, but it allows you access to the lake shore and is available on days when the house is closed. It will take you to the unusual Tennyson Theatre, a little open-air theatre beside the lake, constructed in 1974 by the Tennyson Society at the spot where the poet is thought to have composed 'Morte d'Arthur'. You will come across the occasional yellow post, waymarking the trail, as you walk through the grounds.

The track comes to a small cottage; turn right and through the farm gate to the road. Turn left for a short distance and you are back at the entrance to the Dodd Wood car park.

WALK 4
LITERARY
CAT BELLS AND BRANDLEHOW

(Hawes End – Cat Bells – Manesty Wood)

This is a National Trust appreciation walk! It takes you through some of the earliest properties to be acquired by the Trust and on Cat Bells you will encounter evidence of the practical side of the Trust's efforts to preserve the Lake District landscape.

MAPS:	O/S 1:25,000 Outdoor Leisure Series, 'The English Lakes', N-W sheet.
DISTANCE:	4 miles.
ROUGH GUIDE TO TIME TAKEN:	$2\frac{1}{2}$ hours.
TERRAIN:	A steep climb to the summit of Cat Bells, rough in places with a level walk along the lakeshore (wet and muddy after heavy rainfall).
FOOD AND DRINK:	Dog and Gun, Lake Road, Keswick.
TRANSPORT:	Public car parking in Keswick or Lake car park (see text).
START AND FINISH:	Keswick (or Gutherscale car park – see text).

WALK 4

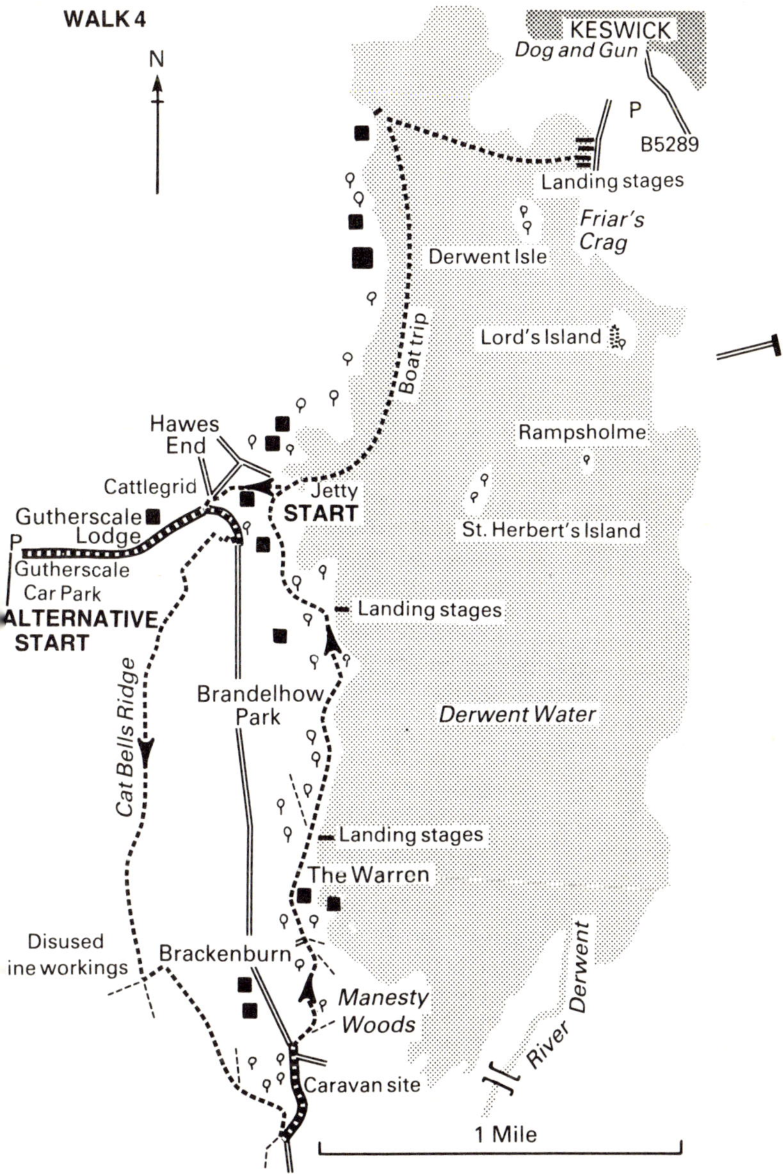
N
KESWICK
Dog and Gun
P
B5289
Landing stages
Friar's Crag
Derwent Isle
Lord's Island
Boat trip
Rampsholme
Hawes End
Cattlegrid
Jetty
START
Gutherscale Lodge
St. Herbert's Island
P
Gutherscale Car Park
ALTERNATIVE START
Landing stages
Cat Bells Ridge
Brandelhow Park
Derwent Water
Landing stages
The Warren
Disused ine workings
Brackenburn
Manesty Woods
River Derwent
Caravan site
1 Mile

ADDITIONAL NOTES:	Keswick-on-Derwent Water Launch Co., 29 Manor Park, Keswick. Tel. Keswick 73013. Launches run from Easter to early November.

The ideal way to begin this walk is by launch from Keswick to Hawes End but an alternative starting point (mandatory in winter when the launches do not operate) is Gutherscale Car Park at the foot of Cat Bells (Grid Reference 246213).

Park in the lakeshore car park, just south of Keswick town centre. The Keswick launches leave at half-hour intervals, travelling alternatively clockwise and then anti-clockwise around the lake. The latter is cheaper and quickest for the purposes of this walk (boat trip lasts about 10 minutes). Disembark at Hawes End and relish the silence after the incredibly noisy boat trip. Go straight ahead to join the main lakeshore footpath and turn right, through the trees and across a footbridge. When the path forks, go right on to a well-made path and through an iron kissing-gate. Turn right then almost immediately left, through another kissing-gate and up into the woods. Another kissing-gate leads you on to the road.

Follow the road uphill, across a cattle-grid and past Gutherscale Lodge. At the road junction, turn left (signed: 'Grange 2½') and follow the N.T. erosion control sign 'Footpath to Cat Bells Ridge'. After 100 yards, a footpath on your right leaves the road and starts to climb the side of Cat Bells. (Note: there may be diversion signs due to erosion control work. Please follow these routes where indicated.) The path zigzags upwards very steeply but you do not have to climb far before you begin to get fine views over the lake. A good excuse for frequent rests.

Derwent Water, often called the 'Queen of the Lakes', is the widest at 1 ¼ miles but has an average depth of only 18 feet, so it often freezes in winter. Directly in front of you, as you look due east, is St. Herbert's Island, reputedly the 7th century hermitage of St. Herbert, friend and disciple of St. Cuthbert of Holy Island. It is interesting to speculate what his thoughts would have been had he known his home was to appear, renamed Owl Island, in Beatrix Potter's *Tale of Squirrel Nutkin.* Farther north lie Lord's Island and Derwent Isle.

The footpath becomes very steep with loose shale in places. Towards the top, you have to negotiate a rocky outcrop. Look out for a slate plaque set into the rock, a memorial to Thomas Arthur Leonard ("father of the open-air movement in this country").

Once you reach the summit, the route south along the ridge becomes obvious. The stiff climb is rewarded with a superb panorama of the northern fells. To the north are Skiddaw and Blencathra, to the south Glaramara and the Scafell range. As you walk along the ridge, the rich pasture and hayfields of the Newlands Valley open up on your right. Cat Bells summit is rocky and can be very windy. Descend along the ridge to a wide, flat area (note the old mine working ahead of you, to the right). Don't follow the path uphill again (ascending Maiden Moor) but turn left, towards Derwent Water, and descend via more zigzags along a well-marked and fenced path. The step-like terraces are further evidence of the N.T. at work. They are designed to prevent harmful washouts after heavy rainfall.

The path levels out alongside a group of larches. Ignore incoming paths from the left and continue to a farm gate. Cross the stile alongside to join the road. This point has a good view of the Jaws of Borrowdale, a scene which inspired wild, Gothic fantasies in the minds of many early eighteenth century travellers and artists. Turn left along the road, passing Low Manesty caravan site. 500 yards farther on, enter the woods on your right via a gate, signed: 'N.T. Manesty Woods'. This is a very old wood, bought by the N.T. in 1908. Follow the cart track, ignoring any paths off to the right, and it leads to a slate-built house called The Warren. The path continues past the house, signed 'Footpath to Brandlehow and Hawes End.'

This path was familiar to the novelist, Sir Hugh Walpole, whose house, Brackenburn, stands less than half-a-mile from this point, alongside the road.

Born in New Zealand in 1884, Walpole was educated at Canterbury and Cambridge. First a school teacher, then a book-reviewer, his first novel was published in 1909. Today he is best known for a series of four novels, *The Herries Chronicles*, which trace the turbulent lives of successive generations of the Herries family, from the eighteenth century to the 1930's. Ambitious in scope, the novels have been compared with John Galsworthy's Foryste Saga. The novels were all set locally and written whilst Walpole lived at Brackenburn. Walpole bought the house in 1924. He was knighted in 1937 and died, unmarried, in 1941. The house is now private and not open to the public.

Fork left past a boathouse and go past a small bungalow, Brandlehow. Turn right through a small gate to re-enter the woods at Brandlehow Park. Follow the path right at the next fork and continue along the shore.

Brandlehow Park was the first property acquired by the National Trust, bought by public subscription in 1902. The Trust was formed by three friends, Robert Hunter, Octavia Hill and Canon Hardwicke Rawnsley. Rawnsley was the vicar of Crosthwaite Church, near Keswick, and one of those remarkable Victorian all-rounders: athlete, poet, writer, traveller, preacher and historian. He was the Trust's first secretary when it was founded in 1895 as 'The National Trust for Places of Historic Interest or Natural Beauty'.

Continue along the shore, through a kissing-gate at Low Brandlehow, and across a field. As you come within sight of Hawes End jetty, the path diverts around a reed bed. The strange, curving bench along the fence is actually a walk-way as the path suffers from frequent flooding. Take the lower path across the field, over a stile and back through the woods to the jetty.

WALK 5
LITERARY
'THE BEAUTY OF BUTTERMERE'

(Buttermere Village – Burtness Wood – Hassness)

Buttermere, surrounded by woods and meadows, is a gem of a lake. The early tourists described it as 'the quintessence of natural beauty' and went into raptures about its pastoral charm and innocence.

MAPS:	O/S 1:25,000 Outdoor Leisure Series, 'The English Lakes' , N-W sheet.
DISTANCE:	4 miles.
ROUGH GUIDE TO TIME TAKEN:	2 hours.
TERRAIN:	An easy, low-level walk, mostly along well-made footpaths and across fields.
FOOD AND DRINK:	Bridge Hotel, Buttermere Village.
TRANSPORT:	LDSPB car park beside the Fish Inn, Buttermere Village (Grid reference: 175169).
START AND FINISH:	The Fish Inn, Buttermere Village.

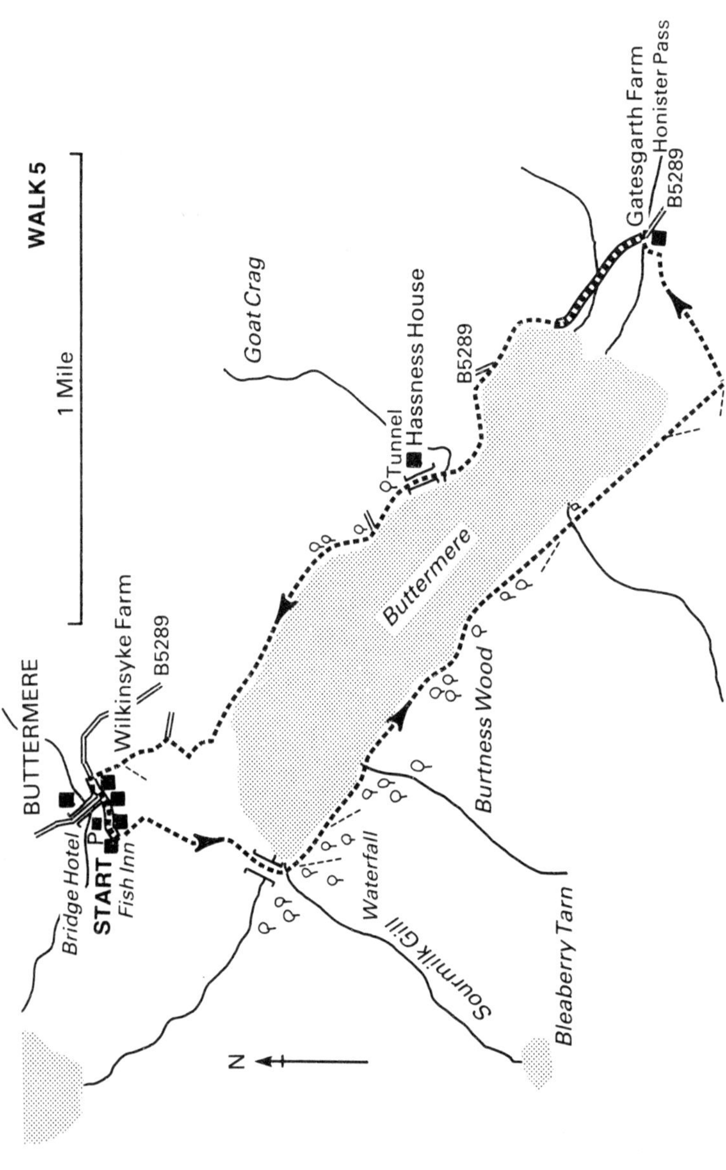
WALK 5
1 Mile
BUTTERMERE
Wilkinsyke Farm
B5289
Bridge Hotel
START
Fish Inn
P
Goat Crag
Tunnel
Hassness House
B5289
Buttermere
Burtness Wood
Waterfall
Sourmilk Gill
Bleaberry Tarn
Gatesgarth Farm
Honister Pass
B5289
N

Leave the car park via the main entrance and turn right past the Fish Inn to the public bridleway to Buttermere.

The Fish Inn was the home of Mary Robinson, a noted beauty in 1800 who embodied the principles of pastoral innocence and beauty which the early tourists held so dear. She was 'discovered' by one such tourist, Joseph Budworth, who gave her a fairly hefty write-up in *A Fortnight's Ramble to the Lakes*, published in 1792. He later modified his eulogistic appraisal, perhaps fearing that Mary's innocent charm would fall prey to the attentions of passing gentlemen tourists. But by then, it was too late. . .

Follow the track to a farm gate and go left, through the kissing-gate. Ahead of you, as you walk between the fields, is Sourmilk Gill, cascading down from Bleaberry Tarn on Red Pike. Sourmilk is a popular name for waterfalls in the Lake District – there are two others, at Seathwaite and Grasmere.

You will shortly arrive at another farm gate. Cross the stile alongside and bear right across the field, keeping the gill directly in front of you. Cross a wooden footbridge and bear left along the lakeshore and enter the trees. Ignore the path to Red Pike but there is another path to your right signed 'Scale Force' – worth a detour to look at the waterfall. Returning to the path, cross a second small footbridge and continue through the kissing-gate and into Burtness Wood. This is a lovely woodland, the predominant species being larch and birch. This lovely, wooded foothpath meanders along the shoreline, sheltered by the trees and with views across the lake to Goat Crag split by the tumbling cataract of Hassness Low Beck.

After following the shore for about ½ mile, the path splits three ways. Take the narrower, left path, over a tiny footbridge (two railway sleepers and a wooden handrail!) and along the shore. As you round the small promontory you come to a superb view of Fleetwith Pike. During the Ice Age this was the meeting point of two glaciers converging from Great Gable and Honister and gouging out the valleys of Gartesgarthdale (on the left) and Warnscale.

Buttermere has a poor supply of fish, but is famous for char. It was char fishing which, in 1802, attracted a gentleman called the Honourable Colonel Alexander Augustus Hope, MP for Linlithgow. His attentions, however, were soon caught by young Mary Robinson. They were married within six weeks and Mary was congratulated for landing such a worthwhile catch. The affair was written about by Samuel Taylor Coleridge, then a correspondent for the London-based *Morning Post.* Following publication, however, doubts were raised by Charles Hope, the Earl of Hopetown, who reported that his brother Alexander Augustus was at the time enjoying a tour of Europe!

Upon their return from honeymoon, the groom was unmasked as James Hatfield, a noted swindler and bigamist. The outcry was enormous, not least amongst those members of the Keswick nobility who were taken in so thoroughly. Employing his talents in the midst of the uproar, Hatfield calmly bluffed his way on to a fishing trip and made his escape.

Into the trees again, ignoring the forestry tracks, and follow the path until you meet a kissing-gate. Go through (noting the modest inscription on the gate) and continue along the shore. Above the open fellside on your right is Comb Beck, another attractive waterfall flowing down between Burtness Comb and High Crag. As you approach the head of the lake, keep to the stone wall on your left and bear left past a sheep enclosure to reach a major path junction. The path climbing steeply to your right leads over Scarth Gap to Ennerdale and Black Sail youth hostel.

It was over such a route that James Hatfield made his escape from the Keswick magistrates. He evaded arrest for two months, during which time the story of 'the Keswick Imposter' caught the imagination of the entire country. Hatfield was captured in Wales and tried for an earlier crime – forgery – at Carlisle assizes. Widespread public sympathy for Mary – whom he had left with a child – resulted in his execution in 1803. Fictional accounts began almost at once. Charles Lamb reported seeing a highly-coloured account on the London stage.

Mary later married a local farmer and now lies buried in Caldbeck churchyard.

At the path junction, turn left, through the kissing-gate and along the track to Gatesgarth Farm. Skirt the farmyard, via the narrow gate on the left, and the path emerges on the Honister Pass road.

Turn left and follow the road. After 500 yards a permissive path (signed 'Buttermere') branches off to the left and rejoins the lake shore. Follow the path across a field bordering the shore. It is easy to see where the lake got its name – 'the lake by the dairy pastures'. Through another kissing-gate and alongside Crag Wood. The shore is a mass of pebbles here and it is *impossible* to get past this point without someone trying their hand at skimming a stone across the Lake (and when one person starts. . .)

The path crosses a footbridge and goes through another kissing-gate (romantic place, Buttermere) and enters the trees. The way is a little rough here, but very pretty and fun for the sure-footed. Shortly you arrive at an oddity – a forty-yard long tunnel blasted through the rock.

George Benson, the nineteenth-century owner of nearby Hassness House, had the tunnel made to complete the circular walk round the lake – the rock would otherwise block the path at this point. It is said he also wanted to keep his workmen busy during the winter!

The roof is low in places, so six-footers beware. Leaving the tunnel, continue along the well-defined footpath, across wooded meadows and through three more gates. Leave the woods via a stile and follow the path back into the village via Wilkinsyke Farm.

WALK 6
LITERARY
GREENHEAD GILL AND DOVE COTTAGE

(Grasmere – Greenhead Gill – Alcock Tarn)

To many people, William Wordsworth *is* the Lake District; the appreciation of one is essential to the enjoyment of the other. Born at Cockermouth in 1770, he spent his formative childhood years at Hawkshead. He wrote about nature and the common, everyday folk of the dales in a way which was revolutionary for the period. He was at his most creative during the years he lived at Dove Cottage, between 1799 and 1808. This walk takes in the setting for *Michael*, one of his best-loved and most moving poems, and concludes with a visit to Dove Cottage.

MAPS:	O/S 1:25,000 Outdoor Leisure Series, 'The English Lakes' , S-E sheet.
DISTANCE:	$3\frac{1}{2}$ miles.
ROUGH GUIDE TO TIME TAKEN:	2 hours (plus at least 45 minutes to visit Dove Cottage).
TERRAIN:	Rough and very steep in places, boggy near Alcock Tarn. A steep descent, rough underfoot, down to Town End.
FOOD AND DRINK:	Red Lion, Grasmere. Lion & Lamb Bar.

WALK 6

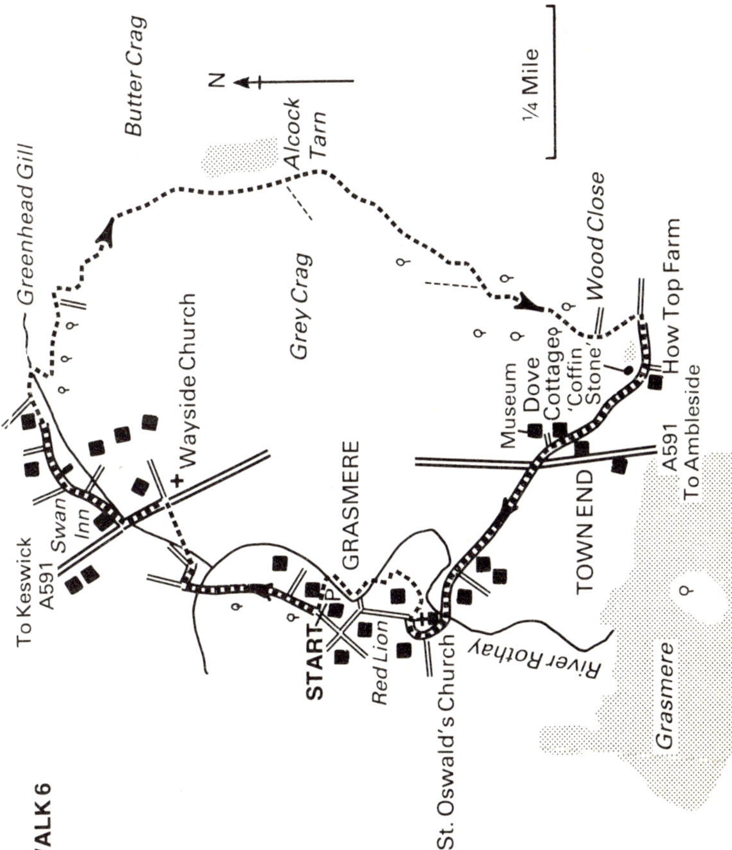

Butter Crag
N
¼ Mile
Alcock Tarn
Greenhead Gill
Grey Crag
Wood Close
How Top Farm
Wayside Church
Museum
Dove Cottage
'Coffin Stone'
GRASMERE
To Keswick A591
Swan Inn
START
P
Red Lion
St. Oswald's Church
River Rothay
TOWN END
A591 To Ambleside
Grasmere

TRANSPORT:	LDSPB car park, Broadgate, Grasmere (Grid reference: 337077).
START AND FINISH:	LDSPB car park, Broadgate.
ADDITIONAL NOTES:	Dove Cottage, Town End, Grasmere (tel. Grasmere 544). Open: April – Sept. 9.30–5.30 Mon-Sat, Sun 11.00–5.30 March & Oct. 10.00–4.30 Mon-Sat, Sun 11.00–4.30.

Leave the car park via the main entrance and follow the road right, i.e. away from the village centre. After a few hundred yards, cross a road bridge and turn right, down a track beside The Rothay Lodge Guest House. Follow the track until it becomes a clearly-defined footpath running between two fields. The path emerges beside the A591, just opposite Our Lady of the Wayside Church. Cross the road with care (traffic can be quite fast along here as locals overtake dawdling tourists) and turn left to bring you to the Swan Hotel.

Known in Wordsworth's time as The Swan Inn, one notable regular was the novelist, Walter Scott. Porridge was the staple diet at breakfast when he visited Wordsworth at Dove Cottage, so Scott used to sneak out of his bedroom window each morning – whilst the rest of the household thought he was still asleep – and repair to The Swan for something more substantial.

Turn right at the hotel and walk up the minor road. At the top of the hill look out for a tarmac lane on your right. Turn up here and continue to the 5-bar gate at the top of the lane, next to a private house called Greenhead Tower. Through the gate and the tumbling beck on your right is Greenhead Gill. Cross the wooden footbridge and follow the gill upstream. The path becomes steep. Keep to the stone wall on your right until it ends.

Greenhead Gill is famous as the site of one of Wordsworth's best-loved poems, *Michael*, written whilst he lived at Dove

Cottage. The story of the shepherd's son leaving the valley for the city, in order to redeem his father's estate, shows Wordsworth's preoccupation with the 'nobility' of the statesman–farmer, over the 'worldliness' of the city-dweller. The exact location of Michael's sheep-fold is a matter for conjecture (it certainly isn't Michael's Nook – a nearby hotel). The valley remains, on a good day, a place of utter solitude.

The path climbs to the corner of the wall, then forks right and leaves the gill behind. This part of the path is very eroded and can be slippery after heavy rainfall. The path continues very steeply up the side of the fell in a series of broad zigzags. Don't cut corners and keep to the path; it is crossed in a couple of places by sheep tracks but they are easily distinguished from the true route – people cause more erosion than sheep. This part of the route is as steep as anything you'll find in this book. Take your time, pause and turn round to admire the view at frequent intervals.

The path climbs to Butter Crags and levels off. The rocky outcrop on your right is a good place on a sunny day for sandwiches and gives a fantastic view over Grasmere village to Helm Crag and up into Easedale Valley (though the tarn itself is not visible). After pausing for views and oxygen, continue along the footpath, past the cairn and along the wall, to your right. Once beyond the patch of boggy ground you arrive at a stile in a stone wall, signed 'Alcock Tarn'. Cross the stile and follow the path round the right-hand side of the tarn.

Just past the tarn, the footpath forks. Go right for a detour to the top of Grey Crag and further wonderful views. Return to the main path, then continue on through the metal gate and follow the line of the wall.

As you start to descend you come to a brilliant view of Loughrigg (officially classed by Poucher as the smallest of the Lakeland fells to be called a mountain). The lake lies below, the island looking almost dead centre (great on a calm day when the lake appears like a mirror). Sheep were once kept on the island, which is now owned by the National Park Authority. Farmers used to row them across in flat-bottomed boats.

The path descends very steeply between two stone walls. The views are good but it is hard on the calf muscles. Towards the foot of the fellside, the walls open out and the path forks. Go right, keeping to the wall until a kissing-gate is reached. Go through and bear left, passing Wood Close on your right. The path becomes a well-defined track and you arrive at a minor road, beside a bench and a sign (pointing the way you have come) for Alcock Tarn. Turn right, walk down to the farm and turn right to follow the road down into Town End.

Just past the pond, look out for a large, flat stone on your right (next to the corner of the stone wall). This a coffin-stone. It was used as a temporary resting-place for coffins as they were carried along the old coffin track to Rydal Church (Grasmere lacked a church yard at the time).

Follow the road downhill to Dove Cottage.

Dove Cottage was originally an inn, called The Dove and Olive Branch, built during the 1600's. William Wordsworth moved here in 1799, together with his sister Dorothy. It was their first Lake District home together since childhood. Three years later William married Mary Hutchinson, a childhood friend, and the household was joined by her sister Sarah. Coleridge used to make frequent visits from his home at Greta Hall, in Keswick, often walking over via Helvellyn. By 1808, William and Mary had three children and the house was bursting at the seams. They finally left for Allan Bank, a much larger, newly-built house overlooking Grasmere village.

William did not own any of his homes in the Lake District. He rented Dove Cottage for £5 a year, plus seven shillings annual window tax. The years at Town End produced some of the best-known and loved of William's poetry. The day to day life of the household was recorded in Dorothy's journal and came to epitomize the poet's philosophy of 'plain living and high thinking'.

The house is now owned by the Dove Cottage Trust and has been open to the public since 1899. It contains much of the original furniture, together with portraits of Wordsworth from the period. Visitors receive an excellent guided tour and on a quiet day – away from the mid-summer rush – it is still

St Bega's Church, Bassenthwaite (Walk 3)

possible to get a sense of what life must have been like there for William and Dorothy.

Nearby is the new Grasmere and Wordsworth museum, a prestigeous endeavour which attempts to place the poet into the context of his place and time (Note if visiting the cottage – return to the car first to change out of muddy boots; the guides have to polish the oak floors each evening!)

Upon leaving Dove Cottage, turn right to join the main road. Cross and take the road into the village. Keep to the main road and you arrive at St. Oswald's Church.

The Church dates from the 13th century and contains a memorial to Wordsworth. It is also one of the few churches in Lakeland where an annual Rushbearing commemorates the day when the old rushes were removed and the floors strewn with new. Today the ceremony is performed by a small procession of children, the girls wearing crowns of flowers and the boys carrying crosses of rushes.

Go into the churchyard and follow the crowds round to the right to a small group of gravestones standing beside the river. Wordsworth and Dorothy are buried here and you can have fun spotting which is which (clue: William had a son, also called William, and his daughter was called Dora). Behind the Wordsworth graves is the grave of Samuel Taylor Coleridge's son, Hartley.

Leave the churchyard by the far entrance, past Sara Nelson's gingergread shop (Grasmere gingerbread is a unique recipe, carefully guarded). Just past the shop, turn right off the road along a track signed 'Riverside Footpath'. This meanders through a wood and alongside fields and follows the river to bring you back to the LDSPB car park.

Sizergh Castle (Walk 8)

WALK 7
LITERARY
RYDAL MOUNT

(Pelter Bridge – White Moss Common – Nab Scar)

Rydal Mount is a fine, elegant residence, overlooking Rydal Water. Wordsworth's final home, it makes an interesting contrast to the simplicity of life at Dove Cottage. It was an attraction for tourists even in his own lifetime as visitors sought a glimpse of the great man. This is a walk which both William and Dorothy knew and loved, a gentle stroll around Rydal Water.

MAPS:	O/S 1:25,000 Outdoor Leisure Series, 'The English Lakes' , S-E sheet.
DISTANCE:	3 3/4 miles.
ROUGH GUIDE TO TIME TAKEN:	$2\frac{1}{2}$ hours.
TERRAIN:	A level, easy walk along well-defined footpaths. Rough underfoot in places.
FOOD AND DRINK:	Glen Rothay Hotel (Badger Bar), Rydal.
TRANSPORT:	Pelter Bridge car park, just off the A591 2 miles north of Ambleside (Grid reference: 364062).
START AND FINISH:	Pelter Bridge, Rydal.

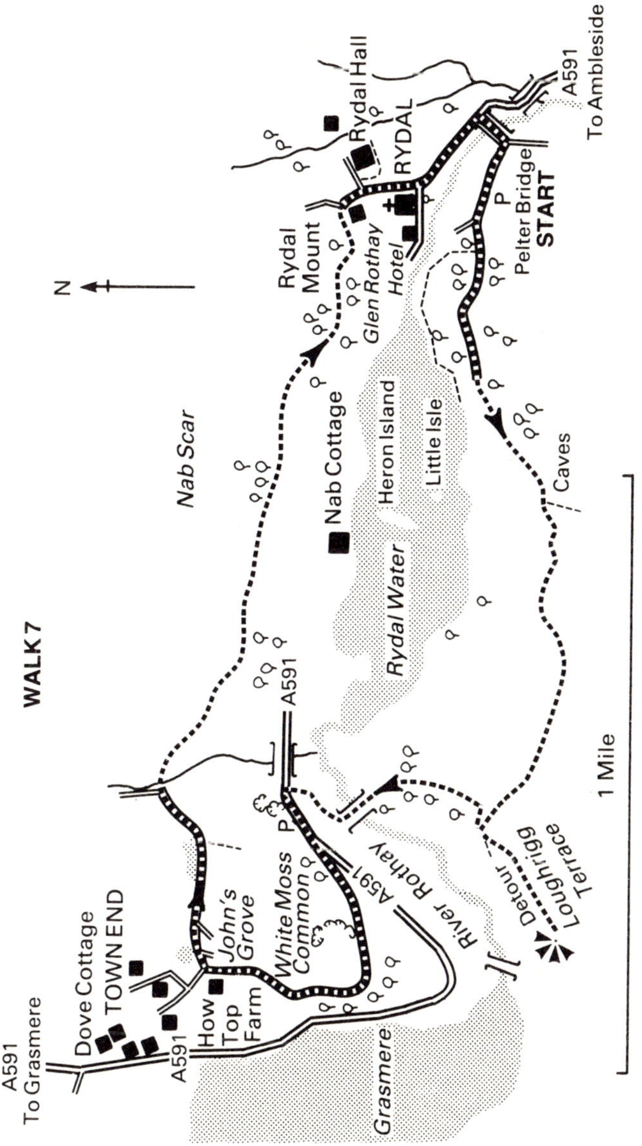
WALK 7
N
Nab Scar
Rydal Mount
Rydal Hall
RYDAL
Glen Rothay Hotel
Pelter Bridge
START
P
A591
To Ambleside
Nab Cottage
Heron Island
Little Isle
Caves
Rydal Water
1 Mile
A591
P
White Moss Common
John's Grove
How Top Farm
A591
Dove Cottage
TOWN END
A591
To Grasmere
Grasmere
A591
River Rothay
Detour
Loughrigg Terrace

ADDITIONAL NOTES:	Rydal Mount, Rydal, Nr. Ambleside, Cumbria (tel. Ambleside 33002). Open: March – Oct. 10.00–5.30; daily Nov. – Feb. Thurs – Tues 10.00–5.30.

Turn left out of the car park, along the lane and past two small rows of terraced cottages, walking towards Rydal Water. The broadleaf woodland along here is rich in foxgloves and is a good area for spotting red squirrels (common in the Lake District where there are fewer greys to disturb them).

You reach a wooden gate (look for the small carved initials of the National Park Authority) and the route continues along a (sometimes muddy) track to a second gate. Go through and the path forks in front of you. The righthand path goes along the lakeshore. Go left, climbing a short rise to a wooden bench, provided so that you can sit and enjoy the splendid view over Rydal Water (especially good early in the morning with the mist just rising off the lake). Directly across the lake is a small white house beside the main road called Nab Cottage.

In 1807, Wordsworth was visited at Dove Cottage by a young fan called Thomas De Quincey. Now best known for his book *Confessions of an English Opium-Eater*, De Quincey idolized Wordsworth and in later life, wrote a wonderful book of gossip and acid memories called *Recollections of the Lakes and Lake Poets*. When Wordsworth left Dove Cottage in 1808, De Quincey took on the lease. He married a local girl, Margaret Simpson, who lived at Nab Farm (now Nab Cottage). De Quincey eventually moved to Nab Farm, though he kept on Dove Cottage to house his books.

Continue along the path, crossing a small beck and climbing quite sharply into the trees. As the stone wall on your left gives out to be replaced by a fence, fork left, bearing round the trees to rejoin the footpath where the stonewall resumes (this slight detour avoids a rough, washed-out part of the footpath). The path leads you to an old slate quarry. There is a small cave here which, although quite safe, is quite a scramble to enter. There is a better one farther on.

Continue past the cave and the path climbs up alongside a large slate tip. As you come on to the plateau there is another, larger cave before you. The roof is about forty feet high and the cave is perfectly safe to enter (but be careful of the deepish pool on the left – you can sometimes spot small fish in here). It provides a good shelter on rainy days and has even been used as a concert hall – students from Charlotte Mason College in Ambleside traditionally sing carols here at Christmas.

Leaving the cave, bear left across the flat area before you and over a small incline. Across the head of Rydal Water is White Moss Common. The dramatic crag to your right is Nab Scar with Nab Cottage below. Continue downhill, the path well-defined as you bear left past the conifers. To your left looms the bracken-covered flanks of Loughrigg. Just beyond the trees, the path forks. Everyone else goes right, so go left, climbing to a ridge on the lower slopes of Loughrigg Terrace. The path drops down to join another footpath. A detour left brings you to a superb view of Grasmere. Ahead of you is the conical shape of Helm Crag (believed by one nineteenth-century writer to be the remains of an ancient volcano!)

Below Helm Crag is a house standing above the village. This is Allan Bank, built in 1805 by a Liverpool merchant by the name of Crump. Wordsworth was horrified by it and called it "a temple of abomination", yet three years later when he came to move from Dove Cottage it proved the only house in Grasmere large enough to hold his family. He lived here until 1811. The house is now owned by the National Trust and rented privately. Until the summer of 1985 it was white but it has now turned pink.

Turn sharp right along the new path and continue towards the river and the woods. (The river connects Grasmere to Rydal Water, which in turn is connected via the River Rothay to Windermere. Wilder members of the local canoeing fraternity maintain that it is possible by this route to canoe from Grasmere to the sea, using the Leven to get from Windermere to the coast.) The footpath meets a stone wall. Continue alongside the wall until you reach a kissing-gate. Go through and follow the footpath through the woods. This path is very popular in summer and has become heavily eroded. The whole of these woods is National Park access land and you will see plenty of evidence of footpath conservation work. This is one of the less-trumpeted aspects of the Park Authority's work. It's Upland Management Service – often in conjuction with conservation volunteers from the British Trust for Nature Conservation – spends many hundreds of man hours each year on the upkeep of footpaths and the provision of signposts and stiles.

The path brings you to a wooden footbridge. Cross and continue along the path until it forks left up to the main road. Cross with great care and bear left through White Moss car park. Leave the car park via the old road over White Moss and follow the road uphill. This road used to be the primary route through Grasmere until the A591 took its place in the mid-nineteenth century. Follow the road for perhaps half a mile, climbing up to a nice view of Grasmere over the wall on your left.

You will come to a 5-bar gate on your left, covered in barbed wire. This is known locally as the 'Wishing Gate', one of many names which William and Dorothy Wordsworth have left upon the landscape around Grasmere. According to tradition, wishes made here would come true.

The grove of beech trees on the right was known to William and Dorothy as John's Grove, after their favourite brother. A merchant seaman with an eye for nature that matched William's own, John perished in the sinking of the East India Company's ship, the *Earl of Abergavenny*.

At How Top Farm, you reach a road junction. The road left descends to Town End and Dove Cottage. Go right (look for the slate sign by the roadside, 'Path to Rydal' and continue up the hill. Just past Dunnabeck, the road peters out to become a rough track and continues to a house called Brockstone. Continue through the wooden gate. The path is rough and can be muddy as you pass under Nab Scar on your left. The path forks at a wall on your left (apparently keeping the hillside in check). Keep left and, after 50 yards, you pass through a gateway.

Follow the path through woods, with glimpses of screes through the trees on your left. Through another gate and across fields and rough pasture with a good view of Rydal Water on your right. The path continues through two more gates and then goes between two stones walls to emerge above Rydal Mount.

Wordsworth moved to Rydal Mount in 1813, following the death of two of his five children. His once-beloved Grasmere now contained too much sadness to bear and when he learnt that Lady Fleming of Rydal Hall had a house to let, he snapped it up. It was a much grander house than Dove Cottage, suiting Wordsworth's increasing stature as an 'establishment' figure. He was Distributor of Stamps for Westmorland (a sort of local excise officer) whilst at Rydal Mount and later became Poet Laureate. The house became a shrine, attracting hundreds of admirers each year. He lived there until his death in 1850 and the house remains with the family.

Turn right, along the road Rydal Hall, once the home of Lady Fleming, who let Rydal Mount to William and Dorothy. It is now owned by the Diocese of Carlisle.

The church of St. Mary (known as Rydal Chapel) was built by Lady Ann Fleming in 1824. William was Chapel Warden in 1833. Behind the church is Dora's Field, now owned by the National Trust but originally purchased by Wordsworth in 1825 with the intention of building a home if he was unable to continue living at Rydal Mount. He gave it to his daughter and although it has a good show in spring it was *not* the site of the famous host of golden daffodils!

At the main road, a short detour right brings you to the Glen Rothay Hotel and the Badger Bar (good bar meals and a nice place to sit outside on a summer evening). Turn left along the road to Pelter Bridge, cross the Rothay and over the cattle grid to the car park.

WALK 8
HISTORIC
SCOUT SCAR AND SIZERGH CASTLE

(Kendal – Helsington Barrows – River Kent)

Starting from Kendal, this walk takes you along Scout Scar, a limestone escarpment commanding fine views of the Lyth Valley, and down to Sizergh Castle, one of the finest National Trust properties open to the public in the Lake District.

MAPS:	O/S 1:50,000 Landranger Series, Sheet 97, 'Kendal & Morecambe'. (The beginning and end of the walk are also shown on the O/S 1:25,000 Outdoor Leisure Series, S-E sheet.)
DISTANCE:	9 miles.
ROUGH GUIDE TO TIME TAKEN:	4 hours.
TERRAIN:	A long, slow climb out of Kendal along farm tracks, easy walking to Sizergh, then across fields and footpaths (occasionally muddy) back to Kendal.
FOOD AND DRINK:	Strickland Arms, Sizergh.
TRANSPORT:	St. Anne's Church car park, Kirkland, Kendal (Grid reference: 516921)

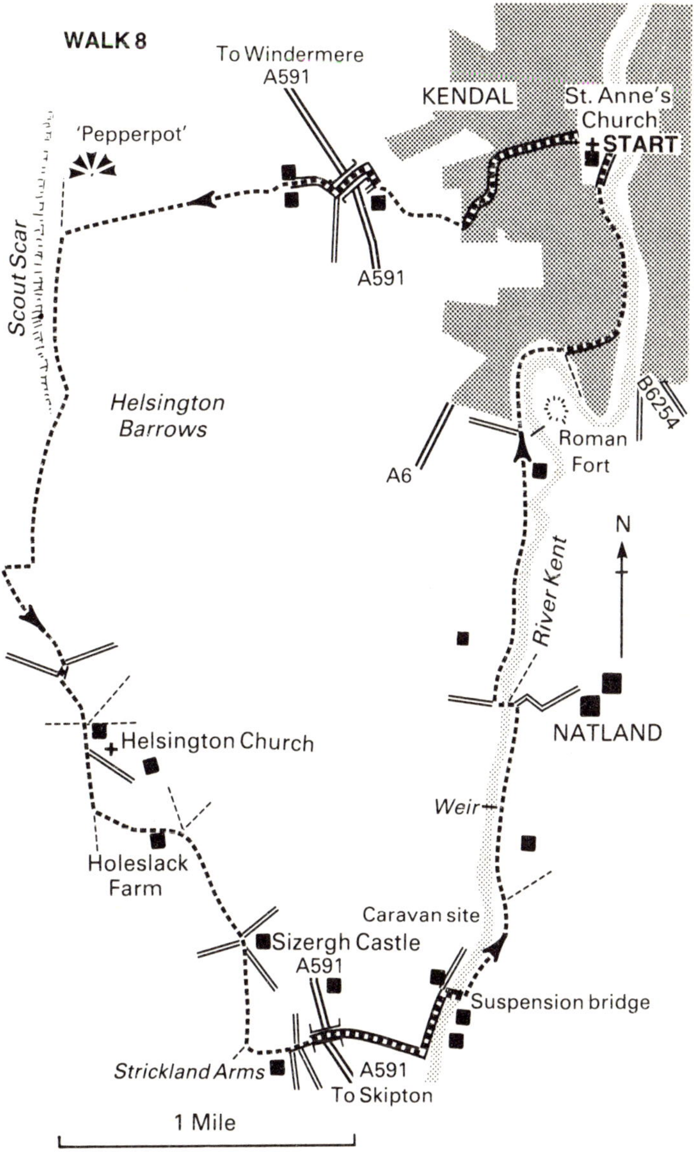
WALK 8
To Windermere
A591
KENDAL
St. Anne's
Church
START
'Pepperpot'
Scout Scar
A591
Helsington
Barrows
B6254
Roman
Fort
A6
N
River Kent
NATLAND
Helsington Church
Weir
Holeslack
Farm
Caravan site
Sizergh Castle
A591
Suspension bridge
Strickland Arms
A591
To Skipton
1 Mile

START AND FINISH:	St. Anne's Church, Kirkland.
ADDITIONAL NOTES:	Sizergh Castle, Nr. Kendal Open April – September, Weds, Thurs, Sundays and Bank Holiday Mondays. 2–5.45 (also normal Mondays in August). Tel: Sedgwick 60070.

Kendal is an attractive, limestone-built town, once the largest in the old country of Westmorland. The town itself features a number of 'yards', the communal building method often found in towns developed during the eighteenth century. To the east of the River Kent stands Kendal Castle, now a ruin but once the home of Katherine Parr, later one of the wives of Henry VIII. The town became famous during the fourteenth century for Kendal Green, a heavy cloth mentioned by Shakespeare in *Henry IV*.

The walk begins at what is arguably the most attractive part of the Kendal, Kirkland Village. Park at the parish church of St. Anne's and walk along the main street, following the one-way system towards the town centre. At Peppercorn Lane, the entrance for the Abbot Hall Art Gallery, cross the road and go through the archway between the buildings opposite (signed, high on the wall, as 'Chapel Lane'). Carry straight on up the hill, past the Pentecostal church and up Greengate Lane. At the top of the road, go along a footpath between what appear to be two concrete caravans.

You emerge on a bungalow estate. Go left, then, after 50 yards, turn right to go along another estate road which ends in fields. Look for a tiny wooden stile in the wire fence, cross and head straight up the field. There is no waymarking and the path is barely discernible. Head towards the line of trees at the top of the field and through a muddy gap, between two iron gateposts. Once through, turn right, along the line of trees, until you come to a gap in a stone wall. Go through and turn right, following a narrow and somewhat overgrown path between two hedges. The path emerges at a cart-track, leading to a group of farm buildings. Go right, then at the tarmac road, right again to bring you to the main road. Cross to the pavement and go left, crossing the bridge over the A591. Once across the bridge, you will pass a gateway and, a little further on, come to a small gap in the stone wall on your right (marked 'Footpath to Scout Scar'). Go through and across the field (look out for the small cairn) to an iron kissing-gate set in a limestone wall. Once through the gate, the path carries on climbing across open moorland, dotted with gorse bushes. Looking back, you have a good view over Kendal. Pass a line of fence posts and head towards a stone wall. Cross via the stile and keep going straight, ignoring any incoming paths. You should be able to see the path winding across the open fellside ahead of you.

As you reach the top of the ridge, you start to get excellent views of the Lyth Valley. Drop down to Scout Scar and the whole valley opens up before you, with the fells of Lakeland in the distance. (If controversy breaks out in trying to name the peaks, a detour right will bring you to the 'mushroom', an eccentrically-shaped viewfinder.) Nearer at hand, to the south-west, is another limestone ridge, Whitbarrow Scar, a rich hunting ground for botanists. Turn left and follow the line of the ridge. Morecambe Bay lies in the distance with Arnside Knott just visible.

Ignoring any incoming paths, continue to the end of the ridge where you meet a stone wall. Turn right and continue dowhill until you encounter a farm gate (signposted: 'Helsington Barrows'). Go through, on to National Trust land, and follow the path across open fellside to meet the Brigsteer road. Turn right along the road for perhaps 50 yards, then, at a sharp bend, take the tarmac lane left (helpfully marked 'This way to Helsington Church'). Follow the lane to the lovely old church which commands fabulous views over one of South Lakeland's prettiest valleys. The bench nearby is definitely the place to stop for sandwiches. Continue past the church and, where the path forks, go right, along a pretty, tree-lined lane. (Ignore the signpost on your right to Brigsteer.) Once in the trees, the path forks. Go left, through a gate marked 'Public Footpath to Kendal Road', and follow the track to Holeslack Farm. (You can see Natland village in the distance – note the church tower.) Go past the farmhouse and bear left past the barns, through an open gateway and then through an iron gate. The track runs out beside a large, corrugated iron barn on your left. Follow the (inevitably muddy) path across the field, heading towards an electricity pylon directly in front of you. In the trees to your left you may catch a glimpse of Sizergh Castle's pele tower. Go through an iron gate between the fields and bear left towards the pele tower and the group of trees. As you approach, you will see a gate leading into the trees to your right. Cross the stile alongside and you are back on another cart track. The right of way crosses the car park and picnic area in front of you. A detour left brings you to Sizergh Castle.

Sizergh Castle has been the home of the Strickland family for the last 700 years. The original house was replaced with a pele tower in 1340, so it is not a true castle. The 60 foot tower is the largest still standing in Cumbria and is picturesquely covered with ivy. The great hall of the house contains magnificent Elizabethan oak panelling and carvings, some of the finest in England. The attractive gardens, originally laid out in the 18th century, are lovely to stroll round on a warm, sunny afternoon. The house and grounds are now owned and administered by the National Trust, though Mrs. Horneyold-Strickland is still in residence.

On a day when the house is open, you could follow the drive down to the road junction at the Strickland Arms. This is by far the easiest route. However, the right of way follows a somewhat devious path across fields to arrive at the same point.

Leave the car park and picnic area via the stile, next to the farm gate in the far corner. Follow the stone wall on your left across a field, over another stile and across a second field until you come to a pair of gates. Go through the stile by the right-hand gate, then turn left and go *down* the field, keeping the woods on your left. Almost at once, you come into view of a farm. Bear left along the wall. The field gets boggy at this point. Just when you think you are lost, you will find a tiny stile, where the stone wall meets a wire fence. Cross on to the farm track and follow it left to the road. On your right is the Strickland Arms pub. Follow the road left and under the A591 (ignore the land left to Low Sizergh Farm). Eventually you will come to a junction alongside the River Kent. Turn left (marked 'Public Footpath – Wilson Place') and follow the road towards the caravan club site Low Park Wood.

Just past the weir you will come to a suspended footbridge. A chilling warning notice advises you to cross in small groups or individually. At the time of writing, this bridge was perfectly safe, though it wobbles and creaks in a most exciting fashion as you cross. At the other side, turn left and follow the riverbank upstream. There is no footpath as such at this point. Follow the riverbank and enter a copse via a farm gate. When the path forks, keep left, over a stone wall and continue along the river, through the trees, until you cross a stile and find yourself on a minor road, beside a road bridge. Turn left, over the bridge and after 50 yards you will come to a sign on your right, marked 'Public Footpath to Scroggs Lane'. Go over the stile and follow the path through the fields alongside the river.

After four stiles leave the river as it bends in a wide loop and head straight across the field, aiming for the telegraph pole. Keep to the left of the buildings, towards the trees and through a gap in the wall. Cross the little bridge and straight across the tarmac lane to a gap in a wooden fence. Follow the footpath through the trees. On your right, in the bend in river, on the far bank once stood the Roman fort of Alauna. You will pass houses and bungalows on your left and eventually come to a stile, next to a sign marked 'Woodland Trust'. A turn right here will lead you along the right of way as it descends some steep steps and follows the riverbank back into Kendal. However, since this is covered in thick undergrowth this route is definitely not recommended. It is also muddy, slippery and generally most unpleasant. Instead, take a detour by turning left at the stile and following a path between two houses to emerge into Bellingham Road. Turn right and, after 150 yards, right again down Wattsfield Road. After 100 yards, right again (this is still called Wattsfield Road) and follow the road until the houses on your right give out and you are back at the riverbank. Descend the concrete steps to a level, fenced path which runs alongside the river.

Turn left and follow the river upstream, past Romney Bridge and back into Kendal. Continue along the main road for a few hundred yards and you are back at St. Anne's.

WALK 9
HISTORIC
DACRE AND DALEMAIN

(Eusmere – Dacre – Dalemain)

Dalemain is one of the finest houses open to the public in Northern Lakeland. This walk from Pooley Bridge reaches it via open farmland and the hamlet of Dacre.

MAPS:	O/S 1:25,000 Outdoor Leisure Series, 'The English Lakes'; N-E sheet.
DISTANCE:	$5\frac{1}{2}$ miles.
ROUGH GUIDE TO TIME TAKEN:	$2\frac{1}{2}$–3 hours (plus 1 hour minimum if visiting Dalemain house and grounds).
TERRAIN:	A low level walk through open countryside but potentially wet and muddy through fields alongside the River Eamont.
FOOD AND DRINK:	Horse & Farrier, Dacre.
TRANSPORT:	Park at Pooley Bridge in LDSPB Eusmere car park (Grid reference: 471244).
START AND FINISH:	Pooley Bridge.
ADDITIONAL NOTES	Dalemain, Penrith. Tel: Pooley Bridge 450 Open: Easter Sunday to mid-October, Sunday – Thursday 11.15 - 5.00

WALK 9

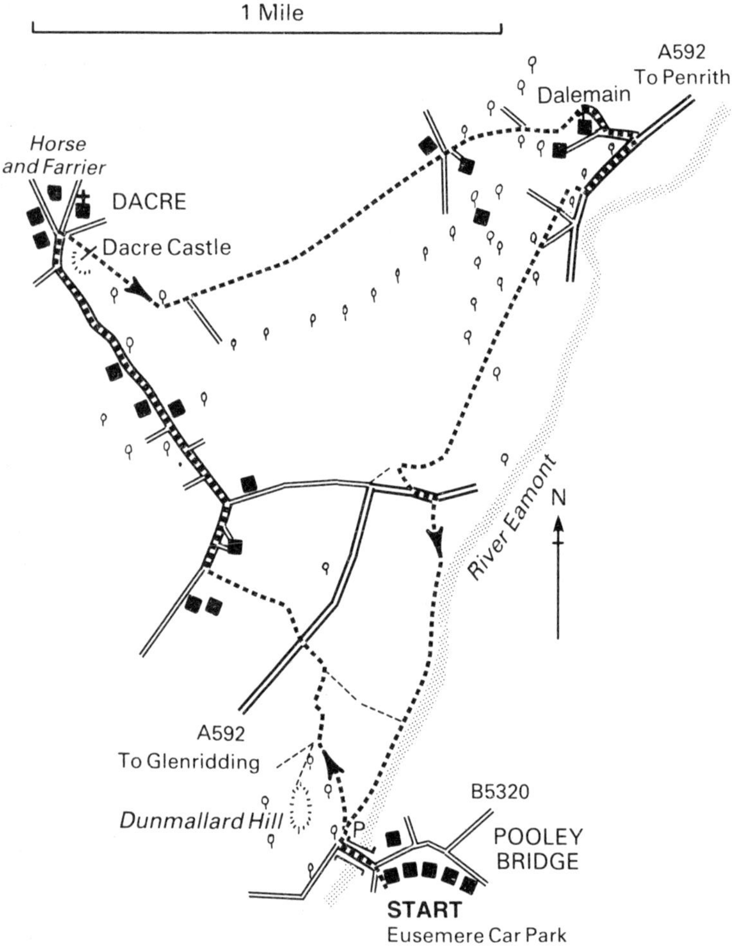

Scout Scar, Kendal (Walk 8)

The walk begins from Eusmere car park at Pooley Bridge. (Eusmere, just to the south, was the home of Thomas Clarkson, the anti-slave-trade campaigner. His wife was a great friend of Dorothy Wordsworth and it was during an excursion to the Clarksons in 1802 that William and Dorothy saw the "host of golden daffodils" in Gowbarrow Park. Thomas Clarkson's portrait hangs in Dove Cottage.)

Leave the car park by the main road, turning left over the narrow road bridge. Once across, look for a kissing gate in the fence in front of you (signed: 'Public Footpath – Dacre'. Go through and turn right, the path running alongside a car park on your right. This is a narrow woodland footpath, heavy with the scent of wild flowers. It is steep in places and can be very muddy after rainfall. The path levels out, with glimpses of fields to your right. There is a kissing gate in the fence to your right, go through and into the field.

The footpath is indistinct here but go straight across the field, looking for a white-topped post in the hedge opposite, next to a stile. Cross the stile and turn left, walking alongside the hedge towards a telegraph pole marked with white. Just past the pole you will come alongside a farm gate in the hedge. Turn right, through 90 degrees, and head straight across the field to another marked stile beneath the group of oak trees. There is no need to cross this stile as there is no fence! Instead, turn left and follow the edge of the field down to the main road and another kissing gate. Cross the road (main A592 – take care!) and go through the kissing gate on the right of the farm gate. Follow the line of the fence across a field, bearing left to a rusty iron gate (signed: 'Footpath to Dacre').

Go through the gate and keep to the edge of the field until you reach the gate at the top and emerge on to a quiet minor road. Turn right and follow the road. This is pleasant farming country, quite unlike the landscape of the central Lake District. At the road junction, turn right and follow the road into Dacre village.

Dalemain (Walk 9)

Dacre is an attractive hamlet, its most notable feature being the church, which is well worth a detour (carry on up the street and turn right at the top).

St. Andrew's church is reputed to stand on the site of a Saxon monastery, known to the Venerable Bede. The present church is largely of Norman origins although traces of the Saxon foundations remain. As you enter the churhyard, notice the 3 feet high carved stone bear on your left. There are three more in the churchyard. Anti-clockwise round the church, the bears depict the following: the first bear is asleep with his head on a pillar, the second is being attacked by a cat, the third is trying to shake the cat off, the fourth bear eats the cat.

(Also worth a diversion is the Horse and Farrier pub. Lunchtime bar snacks are available but there is a sign on the entrance porch which reads: "*Members of the Lake District Special Planning Board, Friends of the Earth and similar organizations are not welcome in this pub".)* Retrace your steps back into the village and just past the farm, turn left (there is a sign, 'Footpath to Stainton', but it is on the opposite side of the road), through the farm gate and follow the track past the houses to Dacre Castle.

This is a fourteenth century castle, on the site of an earlier structure, which belonged to the Dacre family. In 1569, Leonard Dacre led a rebellion against Elizabeth I (unsuccessfully!). The castle, a picturesque building spoilt only by the TV aerial on the roof, is in private hands and only open to the public by written appointment.

The track forks left first past the castle and goes through a farm gate. Through another gate and alongside barley fields. Through a further three gates and then you start to enter Dalemain Park. The tracks leads you into the courtyard.

Dalemain was purchased by the Hasell family in 1679 and has remained in their possession ever since. The pink sandstone front is early Georgian, but the pele tower, built by the de Morvilles, dates from Norman times. The downstairs rooms are open to the public and well worth visiting. Portraits of successive generations of Hasell ancestors are charmingly interspersed with photographs of the present generation. The pele tower houses the Westmorland and Cumberland Yeomanry Museum. The gardens are also worth exploring and don't miss the 16th century barn museum. The current owners are Mr. Bryce McCosh and his wife (nee Sylvia Hasell).

Leave the cobbled courtyard via the archway, walking down the drive to the main road (watch out for deer in the parkland on your left). This is the main A592 again, so take care. Turn right along the road, walking in front of Dalemain with a lovely view of the house and park.

After $\frac{1}{4}$ mile, cross a small sandstone bridge and look out for a stile in the fence on your right (marked 'Path'). Cross the field. Now, the path is less than obvious at this point. Directly ahead is a line of trees, on the far side of the field. You want to head to the left, across to the opposite corner of the field to a gate and a stile. (It is just visible from the road but cows have a helpful habit of clustering there, obscuring the stile. Look for a tall post next to it.) Once over the stile, follow the track, roughly parallel to the road, keeping a wooden fence on your right. The path bears to the right and then forks at the entrance to another field (no gate). Go left, leaving the wooden fence but following a wire fence to a farm gate (look for another tall post). Cross the stile alongside and straight across the top of the next field, keeping the wire fence close by. Straight across the next stile and field. In front of you is Dunmallard Hill.

The path bears right and downhill to a stile. Cross on to a cart-track. The Right of Way goes across this track and ploughs through the middle of a crop field, which seems rather unnecessary. So instead, turn left down the track and through the iron gate at the bottom on to the main road once more. Turn left and follow the road for $\frac{1}{4}$ mile until you come to the river. Look for a stile in the fence on your right, beside the layby (signed: 'Private Fishing'.) Cross the stile and follow the river bank. This path can get very wet and very muddy. It is a right of way across farmland. After a double stile, the path goes left, through some nettles and alongside the river bank.

After several stiles – keeping all the time to the river bank and passing a weir – you finally climb up to a gate and into woods. Turn left and follow the path back to Pooley Bridge.

WALK 10
HISTORIC
WASDALE HEAD

(Wasdale Green – Wasdale Head Inn – St. Olaf's Church)

Wastwaster has a reputation for isolation and grandeur. It is the most haunting of all the lakes, set in a wild, forbidding landscape amongst the highest mountains in England.

MAPS:	O/S 1:25,000 Outdoor Leisure Series, 'The English Lakes' , S-W sheet.
DISTANCE:	3 miles.
ROUGH GUIDE TO TIME TAKEN:	$1\frac{1}{2}$ hours.
TERRAIN:	Level footpaths, occasionally rough underfoot. Wellingtons will be required after heavy rainfall as footpaths are liable to flooding.
FOOD AND DRINK:	Wasdale Head Inn, Wasdale (tel: Wasdale 229).
TRANSPORT:	Parking at the Inn or on the green at Wasdale Head (Grid reference: 186087).
START AND FINISH:	Wasdale Head Inn.

The most dramatic approach to Wastwater by car is from the west, via Greendale (Grid reference: 146086). After a short descent into the valley you are abruptly

WALK 10

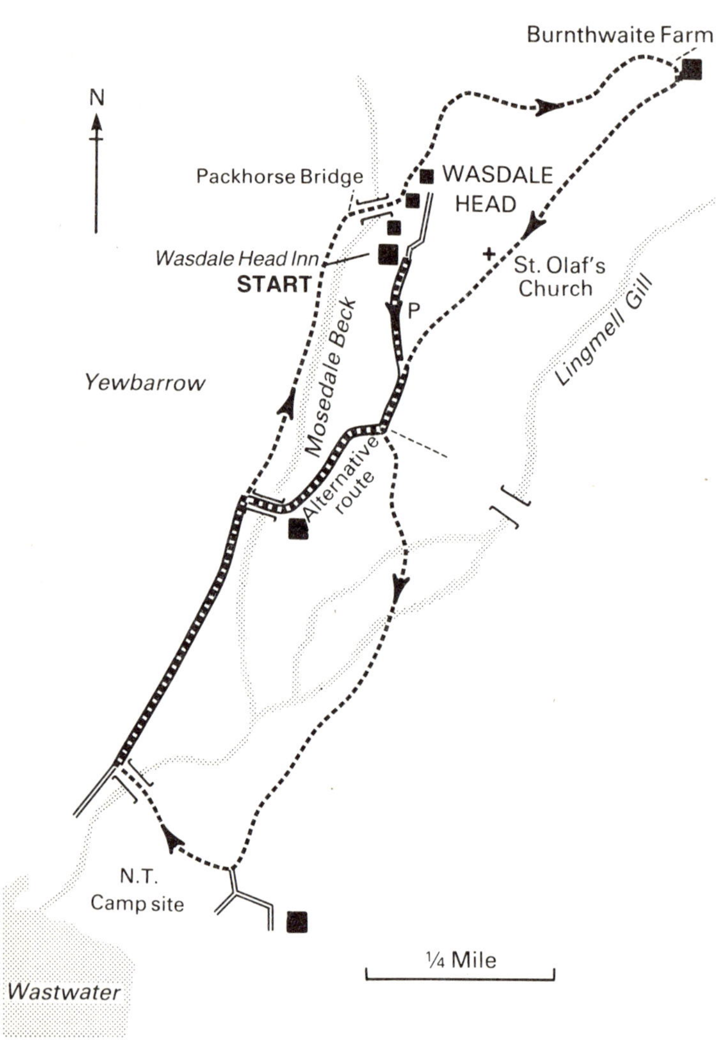

Burnthwaite Farm
N
Packhorse Bridge
WASDALE
HEAD
Wasdale Head Inn
START
P
St. Olaf's
Church
Mosedale Beck
Lingmell Gill
Yewbarrow
Alternative
route
N.T.
Camp site
¼ Mile
Wastwater

confronted with one of the most awesome sights in the Lake District – the famous Wastwater screes. Plunging 2000 feet down the face of Illgill Head, they were formed by glacial action undermining the fellside during the last ice age. Their impact is all the greater on a calm, sunny day when their reflection in the surface of the lake makes them seem to go on forever. As you continue alongside the lake towards the head of the valley you will encounter another familiar view – Great Gable, flanked by Kirkfell and Lingmell. It is the image used as the emblem for the Lake District National Park. The lake itself – and much of the surrounding fellside – is owned by the National Trust.

The tiny hamlet of Wasdale head is popular among walkers and rock-climbers and is an excellent starting point to reach Scafell Pike and Pillar. It is possible, however, to make a much less ambitious ramble around the head of the valley.

From the Wasdale Head Inn, walk back along the road, towards the lake. Just past the green the road bends sharp right and in front of you are two stiles. Go through the right-hand stile (marked 'Campsite') and follow the broad, well-defined footpath across the fields. (Note that after heavy rain this footpath becomes flooded – the alternative is to stay with the road and rejoin the route after the campsite.)

Cross a second stile and keep straight on, over another stile. The path is obvious and bears right through the gorse bushes.

To your left looms Scafell Pike, England's highest mountain at 3210 feet. The poet Samuel Taylor Coleridge made the first *recorded* rock climb when he made a hazardous descent of Scafell Crag by the route now known as Broad Stand. He had pen and ink with him at the time and wrote a letter about it!

You will come to a wide, stony track. During flood conditions, Lingmell Gill overflows its banks and turns this track into a twenty feet wide river! Cross the track, heading towards the trees and the fence in front of you.

Cross the fence via the wooden stile alongside a farm gate and continue into the National Trust campsite to a gateway. Instead of following the track, go through and left. At the T-junction, go right to cross the bridge and rejoin the road. Directly in front of you is Yewbarrow, with the crags of Middle Fell just visible to your far left.

Turn right along the road for almost half-a-mile until you reach a sharp right-hand bend just before a small hump-backed bridge. Leave the road and carry straight on to cross the stile in the wire fence and follow the broken stone wall, parallel with Mosedale Beck. Ahead of you is the magnificent ridge of Kirk Fell, towering impressively above the Wasdale Head Inn. Go through a five-bar gate and behind the Inn to a wonderful old packhorse bridge, apparently held up by moss and weeds. This stands on what was once the packhorse route between Borrowdale and Langdale.

The Wasdale Head Inn has a place in the affections of rock climbers and mountaineers as the birthplace of the modern sport of rock climbing. In 1881, a small group of Oxford undergraduates spent their summer walking and scrambling the fells around Wasdale. The following year one of them, Walter Hasket Smith, together with his younger brother Edmund, began a systematic series of first ascents on Pillar, Great End, Pavey Ark and Gimmer. Rock climbing, as a serious sport, had begun.

Cross the packhorse bridge and go left. The path starts to climb steeply. Watch out for a smaller path going off to your right, beside a small beck. Take this and continue alongside the beck, crossing it several times via a series of small footbridges. (After the third bridge, notice the incredible jumble of stone walls in front of you – each wall appearing to be made of badly-heaped piles of boulders of varying sizes. Not much sign of the stone waller's art here!)

Finally cross the stream and leave it via the path between two stone walls, to bring you out beside Burnthwaite Farm. Turn left and, just past the barn, go right, through a gate and into the farmyard. Continue through the yard and on to the track, over the cattlegrid. Follow the track past the fields, heading back towards the lake once more.

You pass the tiny church of St. Olaf's, the smallest church in Cumbria. It is well-worth investigating this pretty dales church. The rafters inside are supposed to come from the timbers of a wrecked Viking ship (almost certainly untrue). In the churchyard you will find sombre memorials to climbers killed on Scafell, Pillar, Great Gable and in the Himalayas. Services are still held at the church in summer, usually on the second and fourth Sunday of the month. It was once said that St. Olaf's was the smallest church in England (a subject for hot debate).

From the church, continue down the track to the green. Turn right and return to the Wasdale Head Inn.

WALK 11
HISTORIC
CASTLERIGG STONE CIRCLE

(Keswick – Derwentwater – Brockle Beck)

"The full perfection of Keswick consists of three circumstances – beauty, horror and immensity united". This was the view of an earlier guidebook, published 200 years ago. During the course of this walk it is easy to see what the writer meant. From the vantage point of Walla Crag, Keswick has a fantastic setting, sandwiched between Derwentwater, Skiddaw and Blencathra. Friars Crag gives a view straight into the 'Jaws of Borrowdale' and later on during the walk you will encounter one of the most spectacularly-sited stone circles in the country.

MAPS:	O/S 1:25,000 Outdoor Leisure Series, 'The English Lakes' , N-W sheet.
DISTANCE:	7 miles.
ROUGH GUIDE TO TIME TAKEN:	$3\frac{1}{2}$ hours.
TERRAIN:	Mainly along level footpaths but a steep, rough climb to Walla Crag and some wet and muddy fields to cross.
FOOD AND DRINK:	Dog and Gun, Lake Road, Keswick.

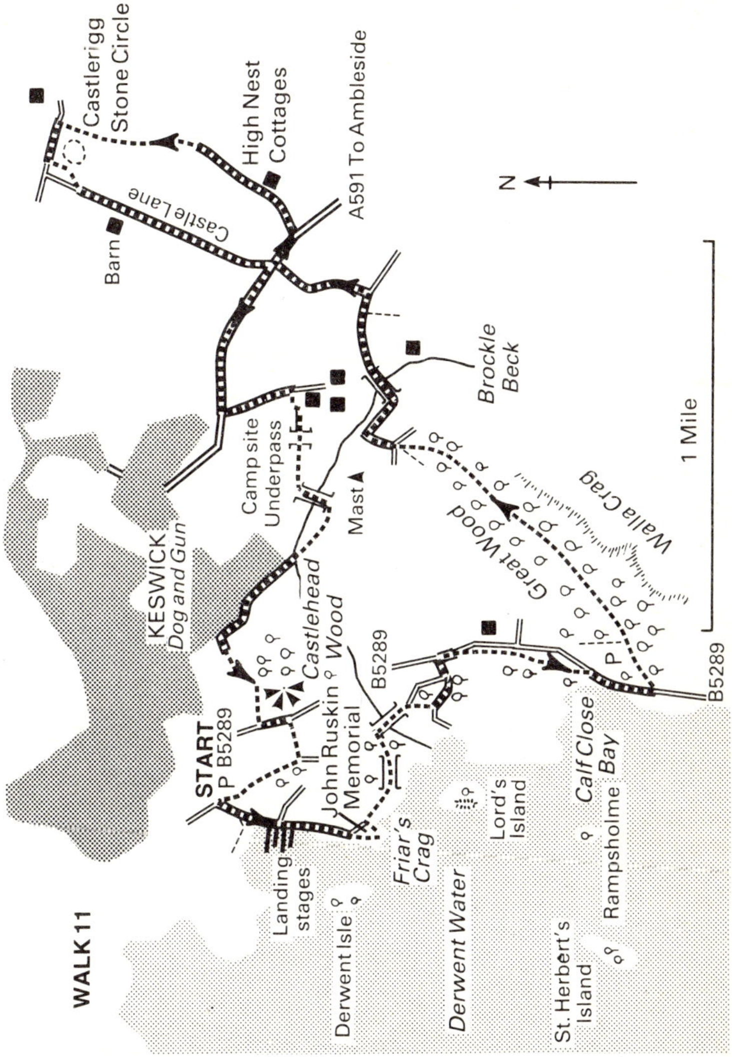
WALK 11
START
P B5289
KESWICK
Dog and Gun
Landing stages
Derwent Isle
John Ruskin Memorial
Friar's Crag
Derwent Water
Lord's Island
Calf Close Bay
Rampsholme
St. Herbert's Island
Castlehead Wood
B5289
Camp site
Underpass
Mast
Brockle Beck
Great Wood
Walla Crag
P
B5289
1 Mile
N
Barn
Castle Lane
Castlerigg Stone Circle
High Nest Cottages
A591 To Ambleside

TRANSPORT:	Lakeshore car park, Keswick (Grid reference: 265228).
START AND FINISH:	Lakeshore car park.

Leave the car park and walk left along the lakeshore, past the boat landings. You enter the National Trust area of Friars Crag. Walk along the track to the end of the little promontory for a superb view down the lake and into the dramatic valley of Borrowdale.

To your right is Derwent Isle, known to eighteenth century guide books as Pocklington's Island after Joseph Pocklington, an eccentric bachelor who purchased the island in 1778 (then called Vicar's Island). He built a house and a series of follies on the island, including a rather fine stone circle. Directly in front of you is Lord's Island, once the home of the Earl of Derwentwater, hence the name; the ruins of his manor house remain. To the right, out in the middle of the lake, is St. Herbert's Island, once the hermitage of St. Herbert, the disciple and close friend of St. Cuthbert (so attached were they to each other that they died upon the same day in 678). Friar's Crag is so named because it is said to have been the embarkation point for monks making the pilgrimage to the island.

Derwentwater has four islands in all, two of which – Lord's Island and Rampsholme – are owned by the National Trust (landing is permitted).

Turn back from the view and follow the right-hand track (passing a stone memorial to John Ruskin on your left), bearing right to the lakeshore. Through a gate and follow the well-worn footpath across the field. The tree-covered knoll on your left is Castle Head. The footpath crosses two footbridges and enters a broadleaf woodland via a small gate (note the sophisticated gate-closing mechanism – good use of local resources!) The footpath skirts the edge of this N.T.-owned wood and passes through a gate to meet a broad track (leading to Stable Hills). Turn left, over the cattle grid to meet the Borrowdale Road. Turn right. There is a footpath running parallel with the road and you should keep to this as the road itself can be narrow and dangerous. The path runs past splendid oaks and, after half-a-mile, arrives at a narrow gap in the stone wall on your left. Don't go through; the path bears right into the woods and curves back to meet the road at an open gateway, next to Calf Close Bay. Go through and cross the road. On your right is a gap in the stone wall, backed by a short stretch of wooden fence. Go through and into the conifer woods.

There is no clear path here. Head straight up the rise in front of you, at right angles to the road, until you come into the car park at Great Wood. Straight across to a wire fence and follow it right to a stile and a N.T. sign – 'Walla Crag and Ashness Bridge'. Cross and follow the footpath uphill until it meets a forest track. Turn right and then, almost immediately, left to rejoin the footpath (signed 'Walla Crag'). You now climb steeply for about half-a-mile, rising 650 feet above Derwentwater along a rough, stony track. The fellside on your right rises sharply to Walla Crag (obscured by the trees) and through the trees on your left you will get tantalizing glimpses of the views over Keswick. The path eventually levels out (one or two good spots for a picnic about here) and then begins to descend once more, shortly arriving at a point where a footpath leaves the main track and goes right. Take the path, which climbs to a fence and a stile. On your left you now have a jolly view of a television relay mast but beyond that is a simply wonderful view of Keswick lying below you. Beyond you can see Bassenthwaite Lake with the vast, brooding form of Skiddaw to the right.

Skiddaw lacks the dramatic crags and angular peaks of the southern mountains being composed of much softer, sedimentary material, formed from mud deposits in the shallow seas of the Ordovician period. Looming above Keswick, 3053 feet high, Skiddaw is much older than the mountains of the central fells – some 400 to 500 million years old.

Cross the stile and continue between the fence and

wall (trying not to be distracted by the view to your left) to a dramatic and unexpected tree-lined river gorge. Turn right and follow the path through the kissing-gate along the line of the gorge. Keep to the path, through another kissing-gate and it descends to the prettily-named Brockle Beck. A very pretty glade opens up before you and shortly afterwards you arrive at a farm track.

Go left (signed 'Path') until you come to a narrow wooden footbridge on your left. Cross and go up the field to the kissing-gate in the wooden fence. Turn left along the track to the lane and turn left, arriving almost immediately at a ladder stile and a kissing-gate, next to one another. The ladder stile itself is a good viewpoint. Looking north-west, you may see a minute white speck half-way up the crag to the left of Bassenthwaite Lake. This is known locally as 'The Bishop of Barf' (it is marked on the O/S map). Legend has it that a bishop once tried to ride his horse up this impossibly-steep crag to demonstrate his faith in God. Not surprisingly, they both fell and were killed. The rock is now kept white-washed by the landlord of the nearby hotel.

Go through (or over) and follow the path (signed 'Dale Bottom') across the field, keeping the stone wall to your left. You arrive at a stile and the craggy, dramatic ridge of High Dod is in front of you with High Rigg in the foreground. To the left are Blencathra and then Skiddaw once more. A stunning panorama.

Continue along the stone wall to another ladder stile, surrounded by signs informing you that this is the path to Castlerigg Stone Circle. Cross and go left. You cross another ladder stile, all the while continuing across open fields and feeling as though you're walking across the top of the world. You eventually come to the main road. Turn right along the A591 for a few yards and look out for the track to High Nest Cottages opposite. Cross and take this track, past the houses to a small wood. Cross the stile, then straight across to the stone wall and another stile. Bear left to a gap in the wall and continue to join the minor road. Go left and the entrance to Castlerigg Stone Circle is on your left.

Castlerigg Stone Circle stands along in a field, surrounded on all sides by high fells. Consisting of 48 stones set in a rough circle about 90 feet across, its setting is truly spectacular. Almost certainly Neolithic in origins – dating back perhaps 4,000 years – its original purpose can only be guessed at. The drama and impact of the site must, however, have lent itself to religious use. It would also have made an impressive meeting place for local tribesmen.

Leave the field at its western edge, crossing a stile to Castle Lane. Follow the narrow, hedge-lined lane back towards the A591. Look out for an iron barn on your right bearing an amazing array of TV aerials. Bassenthwaite Lake again on your right with the conical tree-covered summit of Dodd coming into view. At the main road, cross to the pavement and turn right, continuing downhill for about half-a-mile until you come to a turning on your left (signed – 'Castlerigg $\frac{1}{4}$, Rakefoot $\frac{1}{2}$). Turn up this lane and past the house on your right to a small layby. At the far end of the layby is a small kissing-gate, go through and along the field boundary, keeping to the wall on your left. Look for a similar kissing-gate after 10 yards or so and go through, along a dry path between the farm and a campsite. Round a corner for a good view of Derwentwater and Catbells. A short paved section takes you *beneath* the main campsite track. The path becomes narrow and rough in places, continuing quite steeply downhill to Brockle Beck once more.

Ignoring any tempting paths to right or left, descend and cross the river via a long, narrow footbridge. Turn right to a junction in the path. Go right and follow the stream down through the woods. The path leads you through a farmyard and on to a tarmac lane. Go over the stone bridge and follow the lane back towards Keswick. As you start to pass the houses on your right, you will come to Castle Head again on your left. Look out for a minute sign in the hedge ('Castle Head') and turn down the narrow path between the hedge and fence. Through a kissing-gate and left up some steps. Follow the path to the top of Castle Head for the best views yet of Derwentwater and the surrounding fells.

Descend once more into the trees, bearing left to skirt the contours of the hill and arrive at the Borrowdale road. Cross the road to the footpath and turn left, following the path until you come to a flight of steps on your right. The path runs between two fields to Cockshot Wood. Once in the wood, it forks three ways – go right and follow the path back to the lakeshore car park.

Great Cable from Wasdale Head (Walk 10)

WALK 12
HISTORIC
'LA'AL RATTY'

(Eskdale Green – Dalegarth)

Eskdale is one of the Lakeland's loveliest valleys; its head lies amongst England's highest mountains, its foot at the sea. It is a very lush, pretty valley, best appreciated on foot. It is also famous as the home of 'La'al Ratty', England's oldest narrow gauge railway. This route combines a walk along the River Esk with a short trip on the railway, from Eskdale Green to Dalegarth.

MAPS:	O/S 1:25,000 Outdoor Leisure Series, 'The English Lakes', S-W sheet.
DISTANCE:	$3\frac{1}{2}$ miles.
ROUGH GUIDE TO TIME TAKEN:	2 hours.
TERRAIN:	A level, easy walk but rough underfoot in places.
FOOD AND DRINK:	George IV pub, Eskdale Green.
TRANSPORT:	Car park at Dalegarth Station (Grid reference: 174007).
START AND FINISH:	Dalegarth Station.
ADDITIONAL NOTES:	The Ravenglass & Eskdale Railway, Ravenglass. Tel: Ravenglass 226. The rail-

Castlerigg Stone Circle (Walk 11)

WALK 12

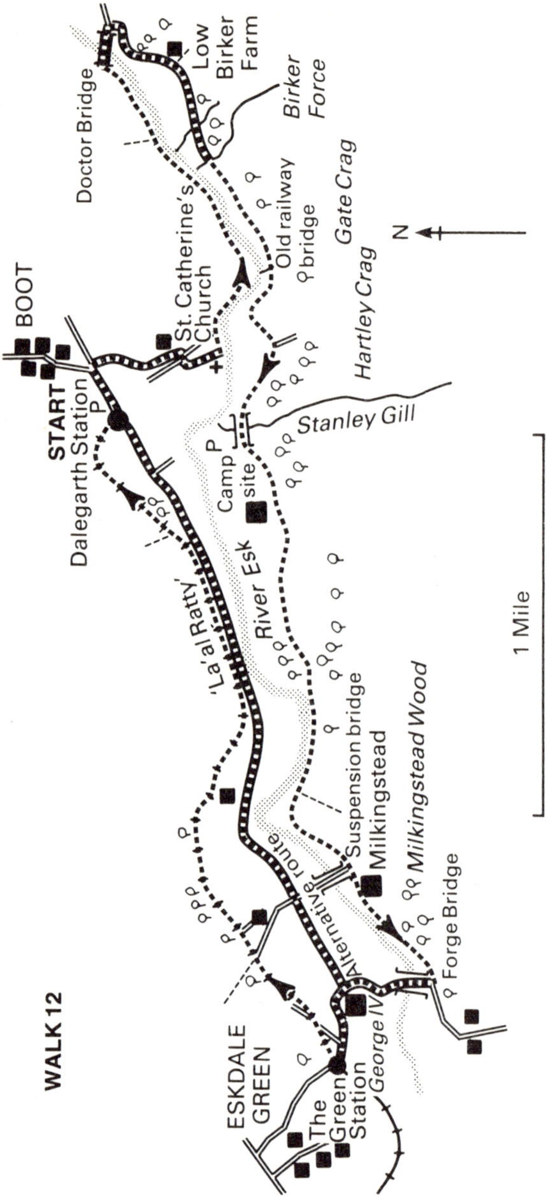

Doctor Bridge
Low Birker Farm
Birker Force
Gate Crag
St. Catherine's Church
Old railway bridge
BOOT
N
Hartley Crag
START
Dalegarth Station
P
Stanley Gill
Camp site
P
River Esk
'La'al Ratty'
1 Mile
Suspension bridge
Milkingstead
Milkingstead Wood
Forge Bridge
Alternative route
ESKDALE GREEN
The Green Station
George IV

way runs all year round, but with reduced service in winter. During the summer, trains run from Ravenglass from 9.10 a.m. until 6.50 p.m. Ask about the 'Eskdale Explorer' ticket. Reductions available for parties.

Park at Dalegarth Station, near the tiny hamlet of Boot. The first thing you should do is arm yourself with a railway timetable, available from the shop. Time your walk to catch a return train from Eskdale Green to Dalegarth.

The Ravenglass and Eskdale Railway – known affectionately as 'La'al Ratty' – is a 3-foot gauge line originally opened in 1875 to carry iron ore from the mines at Boot to the mainline station at Drigg. After a somewhat chequered history, it finally closed down operations in the 1950's. In 1960 it was bought by the Ravenglass and Eskdale Preservation Society and reopened as a tourist attraction. It has been a great success and provides a delightful forty-minute train ride along seven miles of tree-linked track from the coast at Ravenglass to the heart of the Eskdale valley. It makes a splendid starting point for a number of enjoyable walks.

Leave the station and turn left along the road. Immediately ahead of you is an impressive view of the head of the valley with Hardknott flanked by Birker Fell and the flanks of the Scafell Range. Rising behind Hardknott Roman Fort is Crinkle Crags. Follow the road as far as the crossroads at Brook House. Turn right down a cart track, signed St. Catherine's Church. The track runs between two stone walls with a pattern of fields on your right. Just past Burnett House, look out for two giant boulders built *into* the wall on your left (it would probably be more accurate to say the wall was built over them!).

Continue along the track until you come to the next house, then bear right (signed 'Church and River'). Go past a farm and through two farm gates to reach the attractive church.

St. Catherine's is the parish church of Eskdale, built of local granite during the 17th century. In the churchyard is a memorial to Tommy Dobson, Master of the Eskdale and Ennerdale foxhounds. In his time, his reputation rivalled that of John Peel. He died in 1910 and the memorial was erected by nearly 300 friends from all parts of the country.

Just past the church the path peters out beside the river. Turn left along the riverbank (signed 'Doctor Bridge') and follow the Esk upstream. Once through a five bar gate, the path forks. Go left, following the path through the bracken. At the next fork, after a few yards, go right, taking the broader of the two paths back towards the river until you meet a gateway in a stone wall. Our route continues through the gateway but first detour right to the river and a superb little gorge, overhung by trees. There are two iron girders spanning the gorge, remnants of an old railway bridge. This is a good spot for dragonflies.

Return to the gateway and go through, following the path between two walls. There is an imposing view of Hartley Crag on your right. The path climbs above the riverbank. Cross a small beck and go through a kissing-gate, climbing to meet a stone wall and a pair of gates. Go through the righthand gate. This section of the walk commands brilliant views of the fells ahead. To your right, Birker Forces tumbles dramatically through a cleft in Gate Crag.

Ignore the gap in the stone wall, on your left. The track descends to rejoin the riverbank. As you approach a field, bear right through the righthand of the two farm gates. As you continue along the bank look out for a pretty little waterfall beneath the rowan trees where a tiny, unnamed beck joins the Esk. After following the river for about a mile you cross a stile to arrive at a minor road. Turn right, cross the picturesque Doctor Bridge and then right again along the public bridleway (signed 'Dalegarth'). Through a farm gate (ignore the stile in the fence on your left) and begin to climb away from the river, separated from it by fields. The track passes Low Birker Farm, bearing right between two stone walls. Good views to your right across the field-patterned valley. Very lush and attractive.

The path crosses Birker Gill via a footbridge, then continues through a farm gate and straight across a field, past a conifer plantation and a small boggy tarn on your left. At the stone wall, keep left – don't go through the gap – and walk down into the woods, through the farm gate. (This part of the path is rocky and frequently floods.)

As you leave the woods, via a stile, look right through a gap in the trees and you can see Dalegarth Station. Once past the fields on your right, the path forks. The righthand fork is signed St. Catherine's Church and Boot. *Don't* take this fork, go left and cross a small beck via the stepping stones. The path continues across the open fellside towards a larger, older wood. Through a gate in the stone wall and you go through the trees to a large footbridge crossing Stanley Gill. Through the farm gate and straight across the field – used as a campsite in summer. At the farm side of the field go through the gate on to a cart track. Don't turn but go straight across the track and over the stile in the fence opposite (signed 'Forge Bridge'). Cross the field, keeping to the left of the rock outcrop, and then through another gate and into mixed woodland once more (note the pretty farmhouse on your right).

After 50 yards the track forks. Keep left and, after another 50 yards, right at the next fork. The track meanders through the woods. You may hear the cry of buzzards, which nest on the crags hereabouts. You leave the woods and the track descends a rocky escarpment to rejoin the river. It meanders over the heath, then between two stone walls to a pair of gates. Go left into the field via the stile. Straight across to the stile on the opposite side. Along a short stretch of lane and through a gate.

You pass a suspension footbridge; don't cross the river here but keep straight on, over the stile. Keeping to the right at the next fork. You are now walking across parkland belonging to the attractively-named Milkingstead, the large house on your left (these are Milkingstead Woods). The track has become tarmac lane which brings you to the minor road.

Go right, over Forge Bridge and up to the road junction by the George IV pub. Now you have a choice; turn right and follow the road back to Dalegarth, or go left and join the miniature railway at Eskdale Green. The author's casting vote is to go left. Follow the road for $\frac{1}{4}$ mile to the railway station at the Green. Enjoy a pleasant 15 minute railway ride along $2\frac{1}{4}$ miles of wooded track, back to Dalegarth Station.

WALK 13
HISTORIC
WANSFELL AND TROUTBECK

(Ambleside – Wansfell – Town End – Jenkin's Crag)

Troutbeck is an attractive, historical village tucked away on a hillside just north of Windermere. It contains Townend, an exceptional relic of life in past centuries.

MAPS:	O/S 1:25,000 Outdoor Leisure Series, 'The English Lakes' , S-W sheet.
DISTANCE:	6 miles.
ROUGH GUIDE TO TIME TAKEN:	3 $\frac{1}{2}$hours.
TERRAIN:	A steep climb out of Ambleside and across fields which may be boggy at times.
TRANSPORT:	Main car park, just north of Ambleside town centre on A591 (Grid reference: 376047).
START AND FINISH:	Ambleside Market Cross.
ADDITIONAL NOTES:	Townend, Troutbeck, Windermere (tel: Ambleside 32628) Open: April to Oct, everyday except Sat and Monday (open Bank Hol. Mondays). 2.00–6.00 p.m. (closing at dusk if earlier).

WALK 13

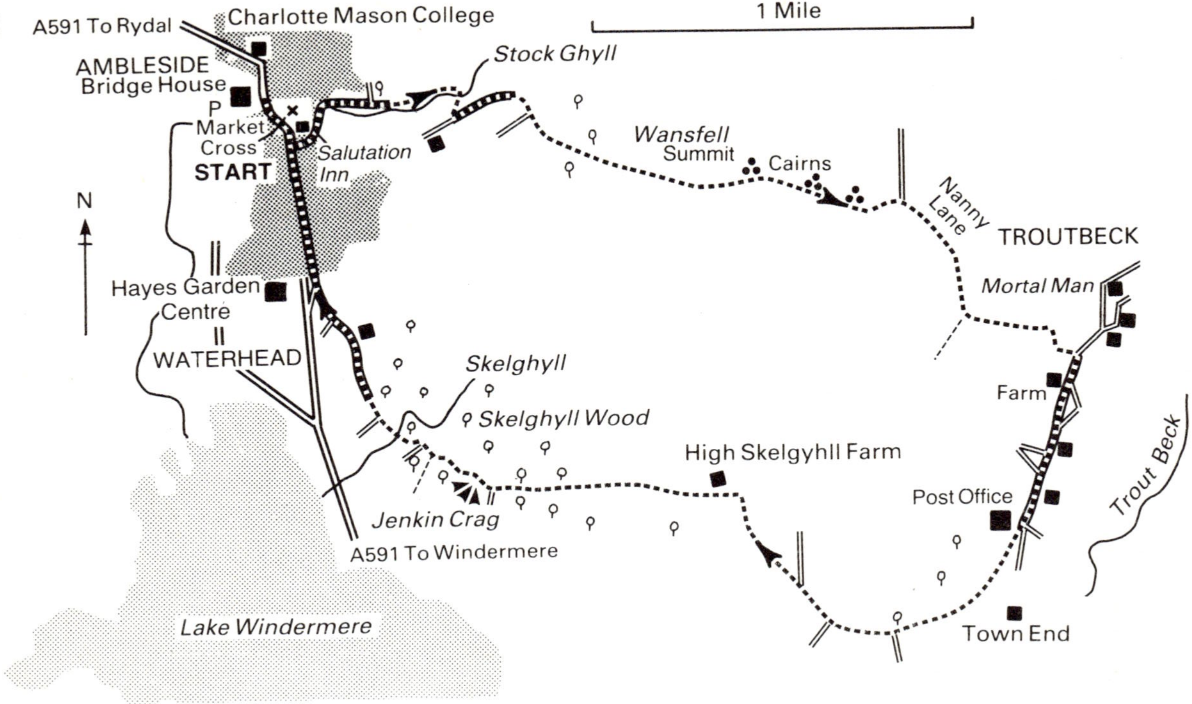

A591 To Rydal
Charlotte Mason College
1 Mile
AMBLESIDE
Bridge House
P
Market
Cross
START
Stock Ghyll
Salutation
Inn
Wansfell
Summit
Cairns
Nanny
Lane
TROUTBECK
N
Hayes Garden
Centre
WATERHEAD
Mortal Man
Skelghyll
Skelghyll Wood
Farm
High Skelgyhll Farm
Trout Beck
Post Office
Jenkin Crag
A591 To Windermere
Town End
Lake Windermere

There are a number of good parking places in Ambleside but the most accessible is the one just north of the village on the A591, opposite Charlotte Mason College. Leave the car park via the tiny footbridge and follow the road back into the village.

The Bridge House on your right is one of Lakeland's most famous buildings. It stands over Stock Ghyll, leading to the legend that it was built by a Scotsman to avoid Land Tax. In reality it was the apple-storing house belonging to Ambleside Hall. It is now a National Trust information centre.

Follow the road to the market cross and turn off behind the The Salutation Hotel. Follow the lane uphill (signed 'The Waterfalls') through a woodland rich in oak, elm and beech. Take the broad track on your left, signed 'Stock Ghyll Park and Waterfalls.' Follow the path alongside Stock Ghyll, past the old sluice gate and over the footbridge. Continue up the steps, following the footpath up to the waterfalls.

Stock Ghyll is a pretty 90-foot cascade, not Lakeland's most spectacular waterfall but delightfully situated and a tremendous hit with Victorian tourists. At one point a turnstile and a charge of 3d were introduced. The beck was important to local industry as the source of power for the three fulling mills.

Continue uphill and cross the bridge. The path bears downhill for a short distance before forking left to go through a turnstile gate and out on to the road once more. Turn left and follow the road to a five-bar gate (signed 'Grove Farm'). Go through and keep on the road for 150 yards until you arrive at a metal ladderstile on your right (signed 'Foothpath to Troutbeck via Wansfell'). Cross into the field and climb steeply uphill, following the tiny stream on your left. The path is easy to see, but hard to follow, being very steep. It gives views back over Ambleside to Loughrigg and the Langdales. The path crosses the beck and continues steeply upwards to an old stone wall (you frequently find sheep sheltering here). Follow the wall for a few yards, then go through the gap and up to a ladder stile on to Wansfell Pike.

This is a superb – if windy – viewpoint with fine views over the whole northern half of Lake Windermere. Looking south, it is possible to see right out to the coast of Ulverston. Much of the peak is National Trust owned and the footpath down towards Troutbeck is well-defined and marked by numerous small cairns. Follow the path down to a stone wall and a gate. Go through and there is a sign on your right, marked 'Footpath to Troutbeck via the Hundred Road'. Do not turn here but continue straight on, following the cairns to another wall. Go through the kissing-gate and turn right between the stone walls. This broad track running between fields is known as Nanny Lane. As you descend you get a good view over Troutbeck valley to Kentmere and Ill Bell.

Troutbeck Village is really a series of hamlets grouped about communal wells strung out along the valley. The farms and cottages date chiefly from the 17th and 18th centuries and are largely unspoilt. Most of them are still working farms and this is a good area to catch sight of sheepdogs 'working' their flocks. The village contains two inns; the Queen's Head boasts a four-poster bar, oak beams and aptly-named Space Invader machines. The other is the Mortal Man, quieter, pleasanter and with an interesting old inn sign.

Descend to Lane Foot Farm and go through the farm-yard to the main road. Turn left to divert to the Mortal Man, otherwise go right and follow the road. Troutbeck has a number of interesting features, not least of them being the series of wells at the roadside dedicated to saints. Look out for them in the wall on your right.

Follow the road for $\frac{1}{2}$ mile until you come to the post office on your right. The return route bears left here, but first continue along the road to Townend.

Townend was built around 1626 and was a 'statesman' farmer's house – somewhat grander and more elaborate than the common farmhouse. It contains fine ornate furniture and panelling and gives a valuable impression of life in years past. Much of the furniture originally belonged here and the garden has been recreated with the aid of an old photograph of

Townend, dating from the late 19th century.

From the post office, follow the track (signed 'Bridleway to Ambleside'), past several pretty cottages. This track, called Robin Lane, climbs the side of Wansfell, past fields and on to the open fellside. Look out for a kissing-gate in the wall on your left (signed Skelghyll and Ambleside) and go through. Follow the path towards the farm buildings, through a kissing-gate and across a beck. Keep to the wire fence on your left and you arrive at the tarmac lane to High Skelghyll Farm. Turn right, over the cattle grid, and go up to the farm.

Continue through the farm yard and on to a rough cart track. There is a good view of Bowness and Belle Isle on your left. The track passes through a gate and into Skelghyll Wood (N.T.). The path meanders through the woods and after $\frac{1}{4}$ mile look out for a sign for Jenkin Crag on your left. Divert to this craggy outcrop for a superb view over the head of Lake Windermere to the fells of central Lakeland. Return to the path and continue downhill to cross a pretty stone bridge over Skelghyll. Carry on down through the trees. The path narrows and bears away from the beck, through bracken. The path joins a tarmac lane by Broad Ings. Go down the lane to emerge at the old road, above the A591. Turn right and follow the road back into Ambleside.

WALK 14
HISTORIC
HODGE CLOSE AND LITTLE LANGDALE

(Shepherd's Bridge – Hodge Close – Slater Bridge – Tilberthwaite)

Hodge Close Quarry has been described variously as "grand and extensive" and an "enormous and unsightly mass of tipped rubbish". Well, on this route you have the chance to make up your own mind. It is a walk through part of Lakeland's industrial landscape, via Hodge Close and the more traditional farming country of Langdale Valley.

MAPS:	O/S 1:25,000 Outdoor Leisure Series, 'The English Lakes', S-W sheet.
DISTANCE:	6 miles.
ROUGH GUIDE TO TIME TAKEN:	3 hours.
TERRAIN:	Fairly easy walking with gradual climbs along well-made tracks and footpaths.
FOOD AND DRINK:	Three Shires Inn, Little Langdale.
TRANSPORT:	Park at the roadside at Shepherd's Bridge (Grid reference: 314998) – turn left off the A593, 2 miles north of Coniston village (signed 'Hodge Close only, $1\frac{1}{2}$').

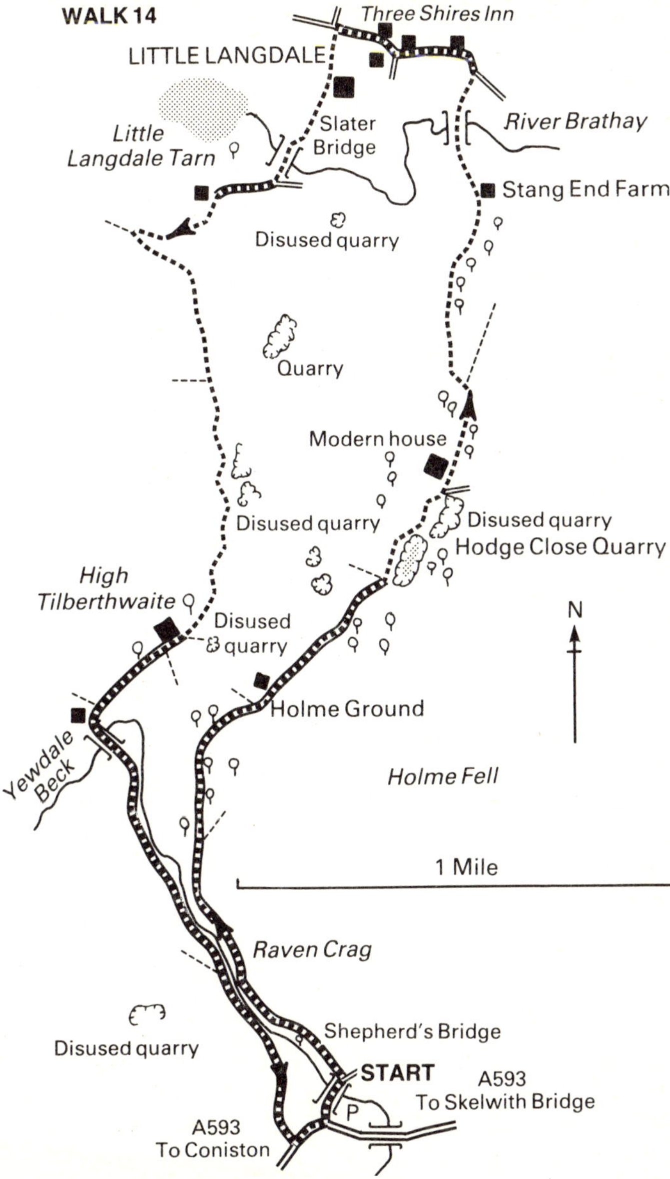
WALK 14
Three Shires Inn
LITTLE LANGDALE
Little Langdale Tarn
Slater Bridge
River Brathay
Stang End Farm
Disused quarry
Quarry
Modern house
Disused quarry
Disused quarry
Hodge Close Quarry
High Tilberthwaite
Disused quarry
N
Holme Ground
Yewdale Beck
Holme Fell
1 Mile
Raven Crag
Disused quarry
Shepherd's Bridge
START
A593 To Skelwith Bridge
P
A593 To Coniston

START AND FINISH:	Shepherd's Bridge.

Cross Shepherd's Bridge and follow the road alongside Yewdale Beck, with Holme Fell and Raven Crag on your right. The road winds its way into the trees, gradually ascending and running alongside a low stone wall on your left. The stones here are worth examining – look for the pock marks left by air holes and bubbles when the rock was forming. Across the valley to your left is an old mine working, the slag heap stained a reddish brown from the copper.

The road enters the trees and you lose sight of the beck. Look out for a classic example of a drystone wall descending the fell to meet the road on your right. After about $\frac{3}{4}$ mile you enter a coppice woodland. Ignore the footpath on your left, signed to High Tilberthwaite, and continue along the road to Holme Ground, a nice old farm now owned by the National Trust. It has a good example of a bank barn. This is also the scene of a small cottage industry, working slate into household ornaments and souvenirs. Continue along the road, climbing past the fields and into the woods again. Follow the road past the line of miners' cottages and descend to Hodge Close.

Hodge Close presents a bizarre landscape – a flat plateau pockmarked by slate pits and old tips. A desolate, craggy landscape but with excellent views of the central lakeland fells. It was a working quarry as far back as 1770. As you walk on to the flat area, the bottom is now filled with water and rubble. At weekends rock climbers can be seen on the crag facing you whilst divers explore the mine workings below.

Follow the road, keeping to the left of the main pit. In front of you is a good view over the surrounding fells – Lingmoor in front of you with the Langdale Pikes and Pavey Ark in the background. The road descends into the trees, past a small house called the Old Forge – now a cafe – and a pair of terraced cottages. As the tarmac finally begins to deteriorate you pass a large, modern house on your left (Wythe Howe) clad in slate which, presumably, was gathered locally. Continue alongside the stream on your left to a farm gate.

Once through the gate, the right of way carries straight on across the open fellside in front of you. However the path is indistinct and the ground gets very boggy. Instead, turn left and carry on along the track, following the stone wall at the boundary of the woods on your left. As the fellside opens out past the trees you get a good view over Little Langdale with the pattern of farmhouses strung out along the fellsides.

Pass through a gate and down to Stang End Farm. Bear left (signed 'Hallgarth') and then immediately right around the farmhouse and through a gate (marked Little Langdale). Continue between two stone walls. Keep your eyes open for sparrow hawks overhead. Keep to the path between the wall and a fence and cross a stile. Carry on across the field to a pretty, gated footbridge. The river Brathay at this point marks the old county boundary between Lancashire and Westmorland. Carry on straight across a field rich in wild flowers and pass through a kissing-gate (alongside a locked farmgate) on to the main road.

Turn left and continue along the road to the Three Shires Inn. This makes a pleasant stopping place for a drink. Sandwiches can be eaten outside or a range of bar meals are available. The pub sign displays the heraldic symbols of the three counties of Lancashire, Westmorland and Cumberland.

From the Three Shires, continue uphill, past a turning left and 100 yards farther on turn left down a track to Birk Howe Farm. Langdale Tarn is on your left. After 50 yards, turn right through a gate (signed 'Slater Bridge'). Through another gate and turn across the field to a stile. Follow the stone wall on your left. It passes a large outcrop of rock, worn smooth and gouged by the action of the glaciers as they passed along Langdale valley during the last Ice Age. Continue down the field to Slater Bridge. This bridge was built for the miners, to allow them to cross the Brathay to get home from the slate quarries. Built along the same lines as a packhorse bridge (no mortar was used originally; the slates were literally jammed into place above a wooden framework, which was then removed). The bridge has been spoilt by the thoughtless addition of an iron handrail.

Continue to the stone wall and through the narrow stile (known colloquially as 'fat man's agony'), crossing a field to another stile. This brings you on to a rough, tarmac track. Once again we deviate from the right of way. Turn right and follow the track through a farmyard (good views of Wrynose up ahead) to climb steeply alongside a slate tip to High Hallgarth. The track levels out and passes through a 5-bar gate. Cross the beck and then bear left up the fellside.

After 300 yards you meet another track. Turn left and continue climbing up the fellside. Through another 5-bar gate. Ignore the turn to the right and continue across open fellside, through two more gates, and the track begins to descend. After half-a-mile you arrive at High Tilberthwaite Farm. Go straight through the farmyard and on to the tarmac road. Follow the road past Low Tilberthwaite Quarry (now a car park). You will pass a terrace-end house which sells teas, cakes and locally-produced honey in the summer. Note its fine spinning gallery.

The road crosses Yewdale Beck and meanders downhill, passing under the flanks of Wetherlam (on your right). Continue to the main A593, turn left and follow the road back to Shepherd's Bridge.

The Ravenglass and Eskdale Railway (Walk 12)

WALK 15
HISTORIC
MUNCASTER CASTLE

(Ravenglass – Walls Castle – Muncaster Chase)

This easy, low-level walk around Ravenglass and Muncaster takes in a rich variety of landscape; river estuaries, sandy coastlines, lush pastures, bamboo groves, a Roman bathhouse and the best view in the entire book!

MAPS:	O/S 1:25,000 Outdoor Leisure Series 'The English Lakes' , S-W sheet.
DISTANCE:	$3\frac{1}{2}$ miles.
ROUGH GUIDE TO TIME TAKEN:	2 hours.
TERRAIN:	Easy. Only the occasional wet and muddy field to negotiate.
FOOD AND DRINK:	The Ratty Arms, Ravenglass (beside the station).
TRANSPORT:	Ravenglass Railway station car park (see text) (Grid reference: 085965).
START AND FINISH:	Ravenglass.
ADDITIONAL NOTES:	Muncaster Castle, Ravenglass (tel. Ravenglass 614). Open: April to Sept., Tues – Sunday (also Bank Hols). Grounds 12.00 – 500 Castle 1.30 – 4.30.

Aira Force, Ullswater (Walk 17)

WALK 15

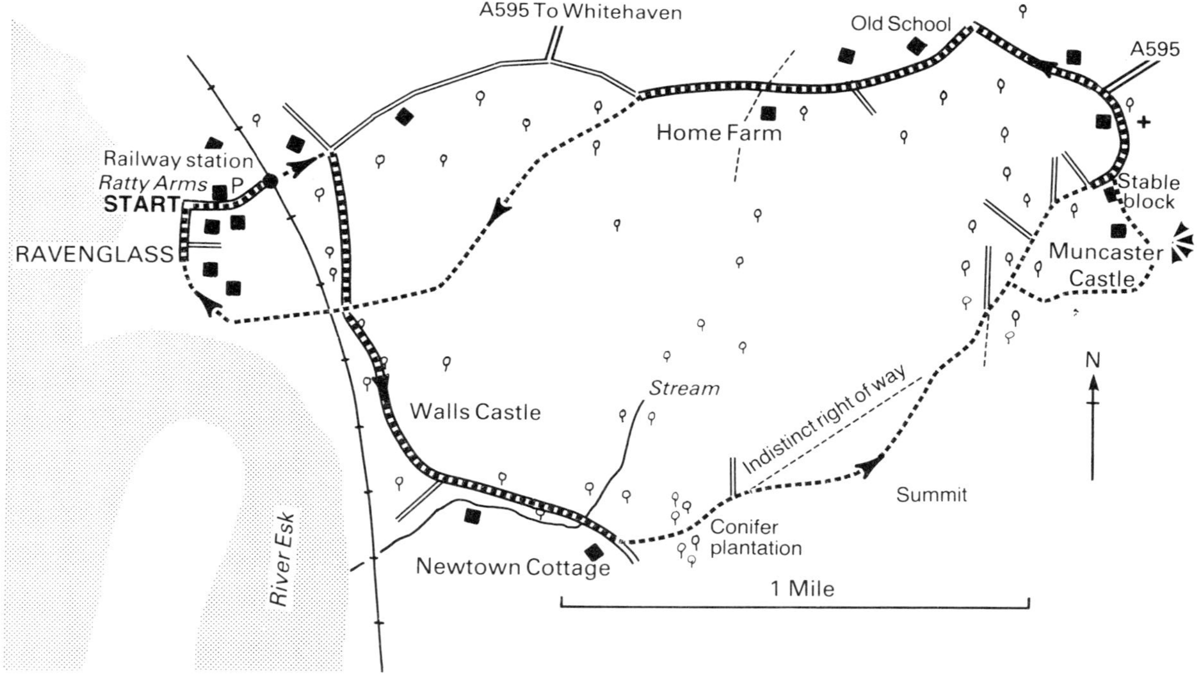
A595 To Whitehaven
Old School
A595
Home Farm
Railway station
Ratty Arms
P
START
RAVENGLASS
Stable
block
Muncaster
Castle
N
Stream
Walls Castle
Indistinct right of way
Summit
Conifer
plantation
Newtown Cottage
River Esk
1 Mile

Park at Ravenglass railway station car park (or, if travelling over from Hardknott, why not park at Dalegarth and take the Ratty down to Ravenglass?). Cross the railway line and follow the tarmac track, signed 'Walls Castle'. Follow this little lane through the woods until you come to Walls Castle on your left.

This incredible building is now the tallest-standing Roman building in the North of England. It was once the bath house of the Roman fort of Glanoventa (which was largely destroyed by the railway line in the nineteenth century) and has probably survived due to the screen of dense vegetation surrounding it.

Continue along the track until you reach Walls Mansion and the tarmac peters out. The track forks (right goes down to the beach). Go left, signed 'Newtown Cottage' and along a nice avenue of trees. You pass a very steep river gorge on the right, heavily covered with vegetation. At the foot is a tiny little beck, out of all proportion to its surroundings. The track bears sharp right, then left and passes a white-topped gate on your left, which should ignore. Continue across the stream with a pleasant view across the estuary on your right. Ignore a footpath sign on your left and continue to Newtown House, bearing left to Newtown Cottage.

As you come within sight of the cottage, look out for a small gate in the fence on your left (just past the rhododendron bushes). Go through the gate (signed 'Permissive Path') and follow the distinct path through the young conifer plantation, climbing to a stile at the top of the field. Pause here and look back for superb across the estuary and, in the distance, the Isle of Man.

Once over the stile, the footpath vanishes, along with all indicators. Use this as an excuse to rush to the top of the hill in front of you, where you will be rewarded with further wonderous views, this time across Muncaster and the river Esk to Birkby Fell. Look north-east and you can see Hardknott. Slightly further left, at the edge of the field, you will see a wood bounded by a stone wall. Head for the gate in the wall.

The gate has a stile next to it, with one of the distinctive LDSPB signs – 'Footpath to Ravenglass' – pointing back across the field. Cross the stile (stone steps really) and follow a clear path into the woods. The path runs through fine rhododendron bushes and becomes gravelled as you walk beneath a huge bamboo bush. You find yourself descending through an amazing grove of bamboo, quite unlike anything else you will encounter hereabouts. The footpath descends farther and you find yourself in the grounds of Muncaster Castle.

Like most of Cumbria's castles, Muncaster is really a pele tower, in this case built about 1325. In the 1860's the fourth Lord Muncaster commissioned Anthony Salvin to convert it into a comfortable and attractive mansion. It is the ancestral home of the Penningtons, who have lived in it since the 13th century. The house itself contains a fascinating variety of furniture whilst the gardens contain a magnificent display of rhododendrons and azaleas. Set against the backdrop of some of the highest mountains in England, they are spectacular.

In recent years, a number of additional attractions have been added to broaden the appeal of Muncaster. If the grounds are open, follow the track right to discover some of these; you will come upon an enclosure containing . . . wallabies. Not often you see these on a Lake District walk! Follow the path round to the front of the castle and a simply wonderful view across the river Esk to the fells of Lakeland. Scafell rises on the left with Bowfell, Crinkle Crags and Harter Fell spread out before you.

If the house and grounds are closed, you should keep to the right of way, which continues across the lawns, past the duck pond to the stable block. Go up the drive beside the stable block (signed 'Church') and past Muncaster Church (notice the two bells on the steeple). You emerge on to the A595. Cross to the pavement opposite and turn left. The road goes uphill, takes a sharp bend left and starts to descend once more. Follow it for about 3/4 mile, past Home Farm, until you come to another footpath on your left, signed 'Ravenglass', at a sharp bend in the road. Cross very carefully and follow the track into the woods.

Cross a beck, ignoring a fork right and go through a kissing-gate into a field. The footpath becomes a bit indistinct here. Head to the left of the electric pylon, towards a small copse of trees, and you should arrive at a gate in the opposite corner of the field. Through the gate and turn right, along the line of the fence until you come to a white-topped gate. Cross by the stile alongside and go straight across the tarmac lane (left to Walls Castle again). The footpath goes under a railway bridge.

The path brings you down on to the sands. Ahead of you are Eskmeal Dunes (a MOD gunnery range – not to be confused by the nearby Ravenglass *gullery* range). Continue along the sands until you reach Ravenglass and the main street through the village.

Ravenglass was once an important port, before the estuary silted up. The Roman fort stood at the end of the route over Hardknott and Wrynose from Galava, near Ambleside. As you walk up the main street, look out for the ramshackle garage on your left, and the old Raleigh advertising sign ("The All-Steel Bicycle").

Turn right just before the Pennington Arms and follow the lane between the houses and back to the railway station car park. (There is only one place for food and drink on this walk; it has to be the Ratty Arms. And don't forget the Ravenglass & Eskdale Railway Museum in the station car park.)

WALK 16
HISTORIC
CONISTON COPPERMINES VALLEY

(Coniston Village – Coppermines Valley – Levers Water)

Mining around Coniston probably dates back to the Romans. Prior to the 17th century, mines would have been confined to comparatively shallow surface veins but by the 1800's iron and copper ore was being extracted from depths of a thousand feet and more. This walk explores Coppermines Valley, once an area of intense industry and now one of the Lake District's foremost industrial archeological sites.

MAPS:	O/S 1:25,000 Outdoor Leisure 'The English Lakes' , S-W sheet.
DISTANCE:	4 miles.
ROUGH GUIDE TO TIME TAKEN:	$2\frac{1}{2}$ – 3 hours.
TERRAIN:	Steep and rough underfoot in places. Not a walk for the ill-shod or unfit.
FOOD AND DRINK:	Innumerable cafes in Coniston village, or try the Black Bull Inn.
TRANSPORT:	LDSPB car park in village centre (Grid reference: 303976).

WALK 16

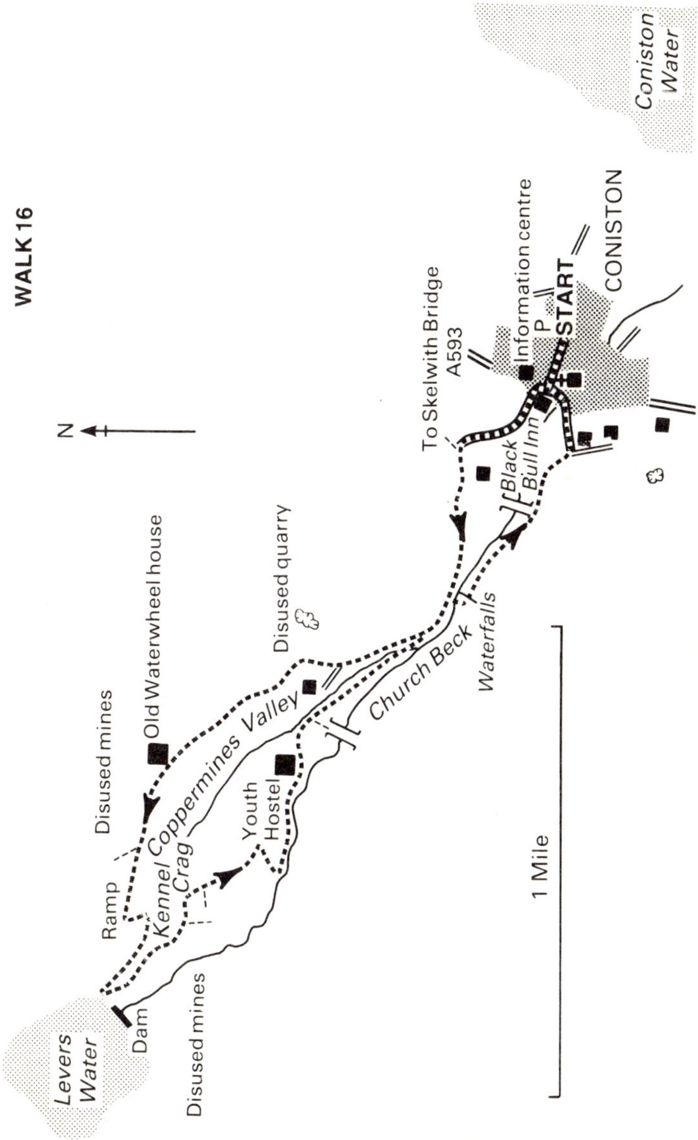

N
Levers Water
Dam
Disused mines
Ramp
Kennel Crag
Disused mines
Old Waterwheel house
Coppermines Valley
Youth Hostel
Disused quarry
Church Beck
Waterfalls
To Skelwith Bridge A593
Black Bull Inn
Information centre
P
START
CONISTON
A593 To Torvor
Coniston Water
1 Mile

START AND FINISH:	Coniston village.
ADDITIONAL INFORMATION:	Coniston Information Centre, Yewdale Road, run by the National Park Authority, is open April to October, 10.00 – 5.00. Tel: Coniston 41533.

Leave the LDSPB car park by the main entrance and turn left, following the road past the church. At the bridge turn right (following the sign for the tourist information centre). Almost immediately turn left behind the Black Bull Inn. Follow the tarmac lane past the cottages. The lane becomes a wide gravel track which slowly ascends and crosses a cattle grid before narrowing. It passes a stream with attractive falls on the right. The wall on your left ends to reveal a small ravine. Church Beck at this point is a stream full of rapids, short waterfalls and deep pools thickly overgrown with aspen.

At the top of the slope the river passes through the remains of an old sluice gate and has a very different profile, gently winding across wide gravel banks. The track similarly levels out and forks. Go right, walking uphill and away from the beck. Looking across to your left you see Coppermines Valley spread out before you. The white building clearly visible was once the mine office, now converted into a youth hostel. The 'gravel' is spoil from the mine workings.

Continue up the track. This was once the mine road and from this point you can pick out the supports for the large waterwheel which drove the mine pumps. The path climbs to some spoil heaps and a small terrace of miners' cottages comes into view. The track bears right. (Incidentally, geologists amongst the party may be lucky enough to find small samples of the so-called peacock ore – the blue-green copper ore.)

The track becomes grassy, crossing many small streams as it climbs level with the youth hostel. You can now see the extensive area once covered by mine buildings (go into Coniston Information Centre if you're passing and look at the old photographs displayed there). To the right, between the valley floor and Red Dell Beck is the straight line of the pipeline (much of it still in existence) which supplied water under pressure to the buildings. See if you can trace the almost level aqueduct which supplied it. Coniston Old Man makes a backdrop to the youth hostel with Kennel Crag to the left of Coppermines Valley – the rocky promontory to the left of Red Dell Beck. The track reaches the old wheel house. (*Safety Note*: do not enter any of the mine shafts or climb on old mine structures!). The wheel house stands about 20 feet high and must have held a wheel of impressive size. Straight ahead is Kennel Crag and a ramp for access to two shafts. Cross the stream and ascend the ramp – another impressive structure with carefully constructed side walls supporting a rubble infill. On no account explore the fenced-off area to the right as this is extremely dangerous.

The ramp is a leat which once carried water to Paddy End Mill in Levers Water valley. Follow the path alongside to the top of Kennel Crag (not a right of way but an obvious footpath). Resist the impulse to explore any shafts, beyond peering into the entrace at the green copper which has bleached out of the rocks.

Follow the path below the rock face and bear right at the fork. Continue steeply uphill to the outflow of Levers Water. The tarn is natural but has been dammed to raise its level. Turn downhill at the outflow, following the footpath. Ahead are good views of the shores of Coniston; the white house on the opposite side of the lake is Brantwood, the home of John Ruskin. He bought the house in 1871 and transformed it into a beautiful home with one of the finest outlooks in the country. In accordance with Ruskin's own wishes, the house is now open to the public and well worth visiting.

The track zigzags down towards the valley bottom, skirting round the east of Kennel Crag. At the fork, go left, towards the youth hostel (the white chimneys are just visible as you reach Levers Water Beck). Pass the powder works and the youth hostel. The track bears gently right. Immediately after the ruined buildings on your right look out for the discarded remains of smelting operations. The cauldron-shaped black residue can be found a mere 10 feet from the right-hand edge of the track. Continue past the terrace of miners' cottages again and look out for a pair of gates. Turn right through the gates and over the bridge, following the track which keeps to the right of the stream. The narrow ghyll is an oasis of different deciduous tree species – a marked contrast to Coppermines Valley.

Follow the track through a kissing-gate and between two moss-covered stone walls. The track steepens and crosses a slate bridge (notice the size of the slates). Cross the pasture land and join the tarmac road via a small swing gate. The cottage on the left serves teas in the summer. The lane joins the main road at the Sun Inn. Turn left and go downhill. At the bridge house cafe, turn left over the road bridge and then straight on to return to the car park.

WALK 17
PUBS
AIRA FORCE AND DOCKRAY

(Aira Green – High Force – Ullswater)

Wordsworth described Aira Force in his *Guide to the English Lakes* as 'a powerful brook which dashes among rocks through a deep glen, hung on every side with a rich and happy intermixture of native wood'. Although by no means Lakeland's largest waterfall, it is the most famous and an obvious stopping place for tourists. Best visited early in the day, to arrive at Dockray village for lunch.

MAPS:	O/S 1:25,000 Outdoor Leisure Series, 'English Lakes' , N-E sheet.
DISTANCE:	3 miles.
ROUGH GUIDE TO TIME TAKEN:	$1\frac{1}{2}$ – 2 hours.
TERRAIN:	A steep footpath to the top of Aira Beck, on well made paths for the most part (rough in one or two places). A gentle stroll thereafter.
FOOD AND DRINK:	Royal Hotel, Dockray.
TRANSPORT:	National Trust car park at Aira Green, $2\frac{1}{2}$ miles north of Glenridding (Grid reference: 401200).

WALK 17

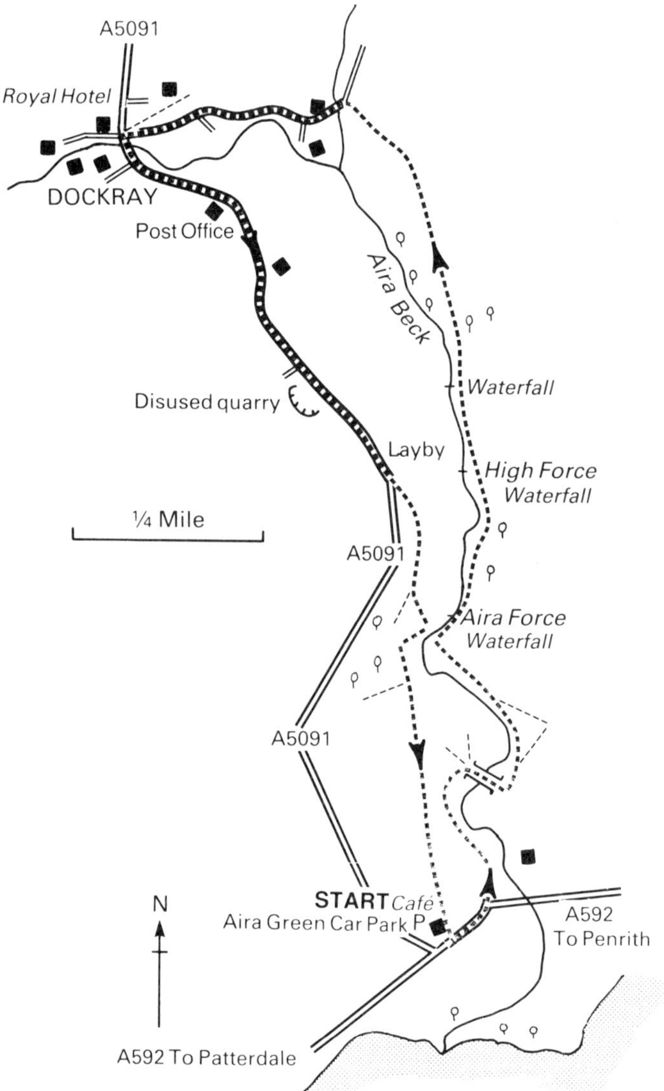

A5091
Royal Hotel
DOCKRAY
Post Office
Aira Beck
Waterfall
Disused quarry
Layby
High Force Waterfall
¼ Mile
A5091
Aira Force Waterfall
A5091
N
START Café
Aira Green Car Park P
A592 To Penrith
A592 To Patterdale
Ullswater

START AND FINISH:	Aira Green.

Park at Aira Green, the National Trust car park $2\frac{1}{2}$ miles north of Glenridding on the A592. Leave the car park via the gate at the northern end (signed: 'National Trust–Gowbarrow') follow the well-made path to a kissing-gate, where you enter the woods and follow the path to descend to Aira Beck.

The name Ullswater is thought to derive from a Norse hero named L'Ulf, who may also have given his name to Lyulph's Tower, an eighteenth century shooting lodge hidden in the trees to the south-east of this point. The tower, which is not open to the public, was built by the Duke of Norfolk on the site of a much earlier tower.

Cross the footbridge, climb the steps and bear left, following the footpath upstream along a beautiful river gorge. The footpath is well maintained and very popular. It is best to get up early to do this part of the walk, before traffic gets too heavy! You come to a fork in the path by a stone bridge. Go left over the bridge for a superb view of Aira Force. Although not the longest (it's 80 feet long) or, some would say, the most spectacular, it is by far the best known of Lakeland's waterfalls. On a busy day the roar of the water barely drowns the click of cameras. Note the stone plaque on the bridge. It was built as a memorial to one Cecil Spring Rice, 'poet, privy councillor and H. M. Ambassador to the USA during the Great War'.

Carry on up the steep steps to your left (with care – the spray can make them very slippery). Pause half-way for another classic Lakeland view. At the top of the steps, the path forks beside a bench and a fallen tree. Go right, towards the head of the falls. Descend to the stone bridge (this one a memorial to Stephen Edward Spring Rice) which gives a magnificent view down the falls to the earlier bridge.

Cross the bridge and the path forks. Go left, following

the river bank once more. The path forks again almost immediately; kept left and go through a small wooden gate (note the high-tech spring mechanism). The path now becomes narrower and can be a scramble in places. At one point it is crossed by a beck flowing over the path. The path eventually climbs to a second waterfall; take a sharp right to bring you back to the well-made footpath. Turn left and, as you come into sight of the river, the path forks again. You want the right path, but first take a detour left down to the wooden footbridge. Note the spring mechanism for the little wooden gate – it is actually a concrete flower pot suspended beneath the bridge! Follow the path until it opens out and the tree cover thins and you come to a broader, shallower waterfall. This is High Force.

Continue uphill until you cross a beck via a tiny stone footbridge and come to a gate in the stone wall signed: 'Farmland. Footpath to Dockray and Ulcatrow'. Go through and follow the rough footpath through the trees. The path becomes muddy and indistinct in places; keep straight ahead, crossing a stream and eventually leaving the trees altogether and crossing a field to a farm gate. The footpath goes left and is marked. It heads back towards the river and a group of farm buildings. Cross a shallow beck and continue along a wire fence to your right.

The path forks shortly before the farm. Go left (signed: 'Dockray'), over a footbridge and past the farm. Carry on through the houses until you come to the main road through Dockray. Opposite is the Royal Hotel, a good place to sit outside in the sun and possibly even have the odd drink or two. They also do excellent bar lunches.

If eschewing the delights of the Royal Hotel, turn left down the road (ignore the sign opposite which says, imperiously, 'Pedestrians'). Go downhill along the main road, past the craft shop and the post office, on your right (only readily identifiable as such by the telephone box in the garden). After half a mile, you will come to a quarry car park on your right. On your left is a small layby and a kissing-gate in the stone wall (signed: 'National Trust – Gowbarrow'). Go through the gate and down the field, bearing slightly left and back towards the river again. Through the kissing-gate at the bottom to rejoin the river at High Force. Follow the path downstream, ignoring the bridge. Note the wooden storm gutters which cross the path at intervals, feeding beck water into the river. Cross the stile in the wooden fence and notice the small dog gate alongside!

The path returns you to Aira Force. Keep to the west side of the river, up the steps and back to the bench and fallen tree. Do not fork left, but go straight on, through the kissing-gate (ignore the path and steps on the left, running along the stone wall) and into the field. Brilliant views down over Ullswater with Silver Crag directly in front of you.

Follow the path down through the parkland and back to the car park.

WALK 18
PUBS
LOWESWATER AND THE KIRKSTILE INN

(Grange Lane – Holme Wood)

Ask anyone to list Lakeland's sixteen lakes and the chances are that the one he or she will forget is Loweswater. It lies to the extreme north-west, only just within the National Park boundary. It is a quiet, gentle lake with some rather good views to the south-east and the fells of Borrowdale.

MAP:	O/S 1:25,000 Outdoor Leisure Series, 'The English Lakes' , N-E sheet.
DISTANCE:	4 miles.
ROUGH GUIDE TO TIME TAKEN:	$2\frac{1}{2}$ hours.
TERRAIN:	An easy walk, for the most part along well-marked footpaths and bridleways. Some potentially wet and boggy patches along the shore of Loweswater.
FOOD AND DRINK:	Kirkstile Inn, Loweswater.
TRANSPORT:	Lanthwaite Wood, Loweswater (Grid reference: 150215).
START AND FINISH:	Kirkstile Inn, Loweswater (Grid reference: 142209).

WALK 18

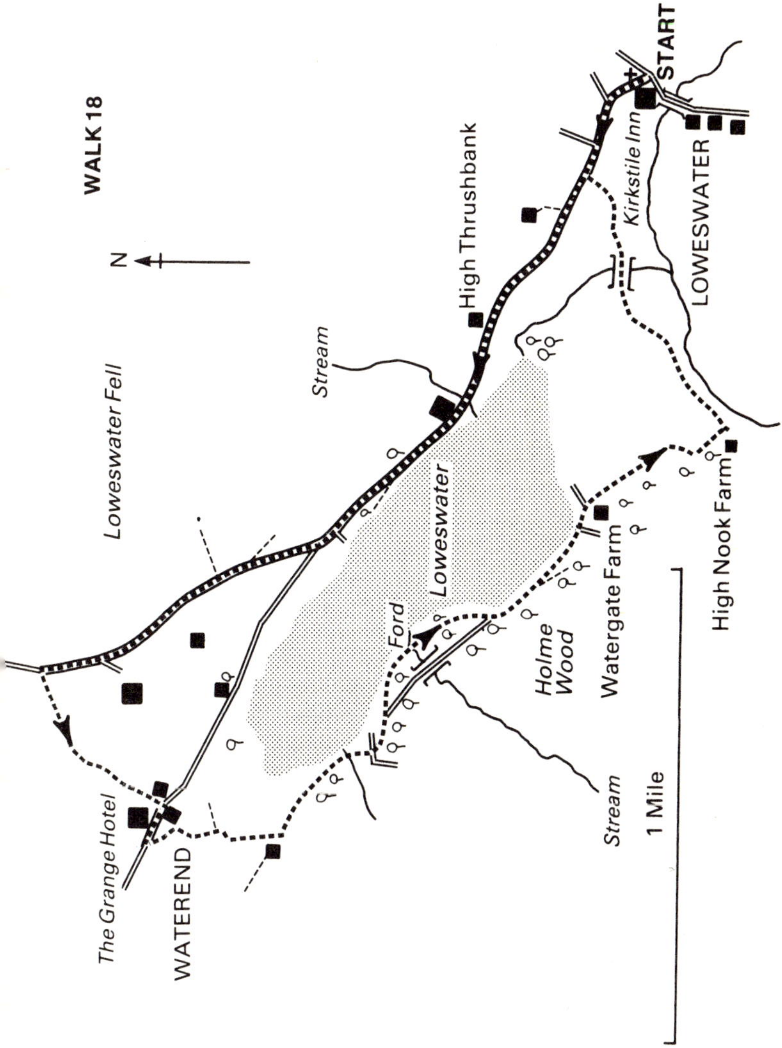

N
START
Kirkstile Inn
LOWESWATER
High Thrushbank
Stream
Loweswater Fell
Loweswater
High Nook Farm
Watergate Farm
Holme Wood
Ford
Stream
1 Mile
The Grange Hotel
WATEREND

The Kirkstile Inn is a very pleasant old inn, with an historic atmosphere. For early risers they provide breakfast – lunches too are good value. From the inn turn left and follow the lane past the church going slightly uphill. There is a good view of Loweswater ahead of you. At the road T-junction turn left past the old school house – now the village hall – and straight on at the next junction, signed: 'Ennerdale and Mockerkin'. Note the small lane at the top of the rise on your left; the walk returns to here! Shortly you come to your first view of Loweswater. Only $1\frac{1}{4}$ miles long, its claim to fame is that it is the only one of the sixteen lakes whose waters flow towards the centre of the Lake District.

Continue straight on down the hill (beware – this is a narrow winding road and large groups should keep well in to the side). At the next group of buildings after 'Thrushbank', turn left through a five-bar gate. This path gives a very short detour to the lakeshore, quickly rejoining the road. 500 yards farther on, at a prominent group of Scots pines, bear right up the fell road (signed: 'Mosser – Unfit for Cars'). Go uphill, ignoring the gated track on your left as you ascend the lane, going up the side of Loweswater Fell. The effort of getting up is rewarded with grand views of Loweswater set against a background of fells (interestingly enough, you can look across to *another* Loweswater Fell, just to the right of Mellbreak.) Continuing up the fell road, there are good views out across the vale to the coast and, on a good day, the Isle of Man.

The road levels out and bears right around the contour of the hill. The next footpath sign is visible from a long way off. Turn left at the sign (marked – indistinctly! – 'Loweswater Road'). Carry on downhill to a farm gate. Follow the track. Note the clapper-type bridge on the way down. The Lane reaches Grange Road via an attractive farmstead – look, for instance, at the stone trough and the roof over the front door. Turn right towards the Grange Hotel. As you pass the second entrance to the hotel (on your right), go left, following a waymarked bridleway (to Hudson Place Farm). A little away along the track you meet a cattle grid – the rollers are unsafe (they really roll!), so go through the gate alongside.

This is a walk of ignoring incoming footpaths; this time a path comes in from the left. You have a nice view of Mellbreak and Crummock Water. The track leads to a farmhouse with an attractive shield/crest featuring a white bull. The tarmac track leads into the farmyard but you should follow the short section of gravelled track to a pair of five-bar gates. Take the left gate, between two stone walls. Shortly you come to another gate and the stone walls continue for a short distance beyond. The track arrives at the lakeshore. This is a nice, grassy path alongside the reed beds at the edge of the woods. The track crosses a stream before coming to a neat stone stile built into a wall, with a gate for horses alongside. Go into the wood.

This is Holme Wood, owned by the National Trust. A pleasant mixed woodland, the presence of trees gives Loweswater its name, which means simply 'the leafy lake'. Cross a stream and the footpath bears left away from the bridleway and meanders down to the lakeshore. You have to ford a shallow stream – if footwear is unsuitable, stick to the bridleway. Keeping to the lakeshore path, just past a woodman's cottage you rejoin the bridleway. Cross another stream and bear left at the next fork, through a grove of impressive beeches to a pair of five-bar gates which lead you to Watergate Farm.

Look for a five-bar gate to the right of the barn with the dovecot and take the permissive path to High Nook Farm (N.T.) The path follows the fence to a stile. Go over the stile, keeping the fence to your left until you reach the next stile. You come to a wide field with a wall on the opposite side. A sturdy ladder stile lies just out of sight around the contour of the hill. Keep to the higher ground – keeping the copse to your right – and cross the stile.

The path joins the farm track from High Nook. Turn left and follow the track down the slope, beside a stream. Pass through two five-bar gates in quick succession and then bear right on to the tarmac road. Walk up to the main road, turn right to the school house again and follow the road back to the Kirkstile Inn, enjoying the views of Crummock Water and the Borrowdale Valley, with Mellbreak rising impressively behind the Kirkstile Inn.

WALK 19
PUBS
SCHOOL KNOTT AND THE HOLE INT' WALL

(Bowness – Matson Ground – Lickbarrow)

MAPS:	O/S 1:25,000 Outdoor Leisure Series, 'The English Lakes' , S-E sheet.
DISTANCE:	$5\frac{1}{2}$ miles.
ROUGH GUIDE TO TIME TAKEN:	$2\frac{1}{2}$ hours.
TERRAIN:	A moderate climb out of Bowness, thereafter over undulating countryside, along fields, country lanes and the occasional muddy footpath.
FOOD AND DRINK:	Hole Int' Wall pub, Fallbarrow Road, Bowness.
TRANSPORT:	Public car park, Rayrigg Road, Bowness. (Grid reference: 403973)
START AND FINISH:	Hole Int' Wall, Bowness.

The oldest part of Bowness (pronounced locally as 'Bonus') is Lowside, the ancient muddle of streets and cottages behind St. Martin's Church. This area used to contain the saw pit, the smithy, and two of the three inns which stood along the original road through the village.

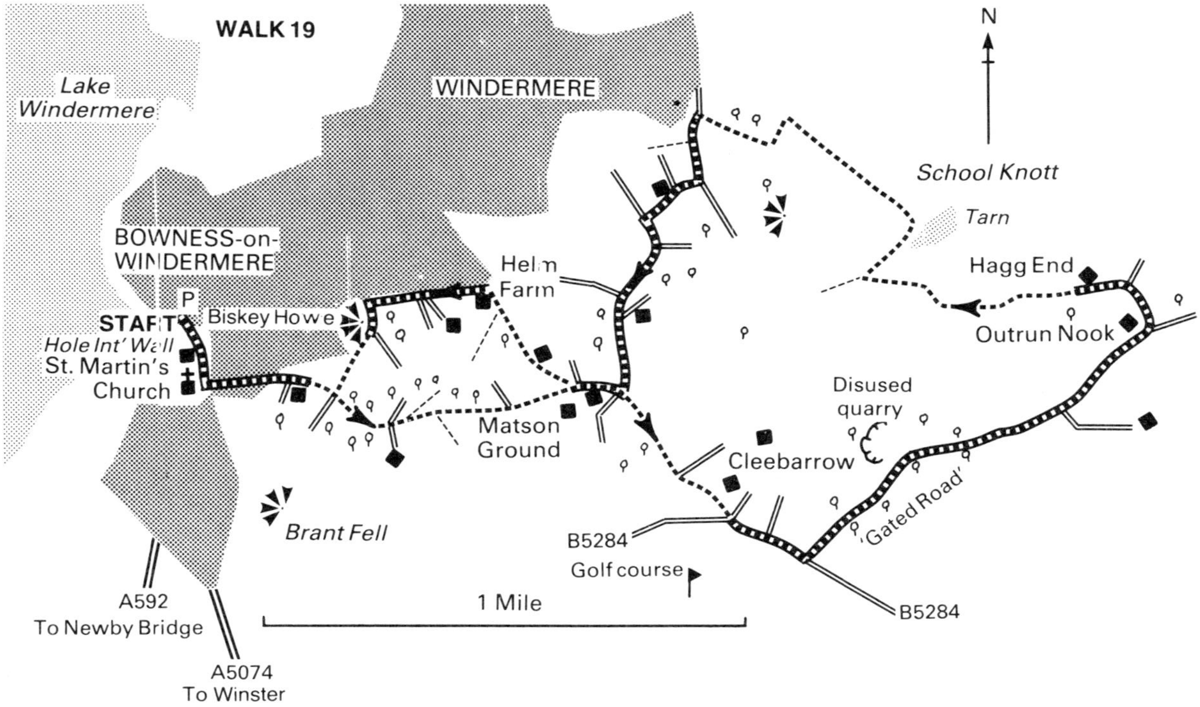
WALK 19
N
Lake Windermere
WINDERMERE
BOWNESS-on-WINDERMERE
P
START
Hole Int' Wall
St. Martin's Church
Biskey Howe
Helm Farm
Matson Ground
School Knott
Tarn
Hagg End
Outrun Nook
Disused quarry
Cleebarrow
'Gated Road'
Brant Fell
B5284
Golf course
B5284
1 Mile
A592
To Newby Bridge
A5074
To Winster

The New Hall Inn, known as The Hole Int' Wall – presumably because ale could be handed directly through a window to the smithy next door – is arguably the oldest of them. A quaint old pub of real character, it is much favoured by locals and visitors alike. Charles Dickens once drank here during a walking tour of the lakes.

To reach the pub from the car park, leave via the Fallbarrow Road exit, next to the craft centre, and turn left. Time this walk right and you should be back by lunchtime opening! Continue past the Hole Int' Wall and bear right towards the Church.

St. Martin's Church is well-worth close inspection. St. Martin was a Roman soldier who shared his cloak with a beggar. The present church was originally built in 1483, on the site of a much earlier church which had been destroyed by fire. It later suffered at the hands of Victorian 'improvers'. The stained-glass windows are particularly fine. One feature of special interest to American visitors is the family coat of arms of George Washington in one corner of the East Window. This was later incorporated into the Stars and Stripes.

Bear left past the church, cross the main road and walk up Kendal Road opposite, turning left after 100 yards or so and climbing up Brantfell Road. At the top of this narrow lane, go through an iron gate and into a field. This gate marks the end of the Dales Way and you will encounter the distinctive yellow arrows waymarking the route throughout this walk.

Go straight up the field and through a kissing-gate at the top, on to a track. This track goes left to Biskey Howe, a well-known local viewpoint, and right to Brantfell. Straight across, however, is another kissing-gate, marked 'Matson Ground and Cleanborrow'. Go through and follow the stone wall on your left across the field. Ignore the gap in the wall and continue to the corner of the field and a small iron gate. The path continues between two stone walls, crossing a tarmac drive en route. You are already walking in pleasant, open country–side and the crowds and traffic of Bowness feel a hundred miles away.

The path passes to the right of a farm gate and through a small iron gate. Keep to the stone wall on your right and through another iron gate beside a large sycamore tree. Into the next field and the path becomes indistinct. Bear diagonally left, aiming to the *right* of a group of Scots pine, and you will meet yet another iron gate set in a stone wall. Beyond this you will meet a tarmac road. Turn right for 20 yards. Matson Ground is the large white house in the trees in front of you. At the distinctive, hand-painted sign, rejoin the footpath on your left and go through a kissing-gate. The path now goes right, crossing the field and keeping close to the stone wall. Through another kissing-gate and turn right through the next field, passing a Dales Way sign, to emerge on to a tarmac drive leading to Matson Ground.

Cross the drive to a fence, through another kissing-gate (you have to look very carefully for the tiny footpath sign) and turn right along the line of the fence. You come to a LDSPB kissing-gate and go through on to Lickbarrow Road, next to the entrance to Matson Ground. Straight across the road to another kissing-gate. This is marked with the Dales Way symbol. Look to your right and Brantfell is visible; this viewpoint gives an excellent view down the southern length of Lake Windermere. The path crosses the next field, bearing right through a small group of firs. It becomes indistinct so you should head towards the top right-hand corner of the field where you will find yet another kissing-gate in a stone wall. The footpath goes straight up the next field. Note the huge arrows painted on the trees to left and right – just to make sure you don't wander from your route! At the top of the rise, bear right and through a kissing-gate to turn left between the wall and wire fence to another kissing-gate. Follow the stone wall on your left to an extremely well-sprung gate and on to a tarmac drive (leading to Cleabarrow). Turn right to the road.

You come on to the B5284 just above the entrance to Windermere golf club. Turn left and walk along the road for perhaps 300 yards, passing one turning and coming to another, marked 'Gated Road'. Turn left up here and you start to walk along a pretty country lane with good views ahead of you towards the Kentmere Valley.

Keeping to the road, you go through several gates to reach a farm, romantically-named (on the O/S map at any rate) Outrun Nook. Keep to the road, going past the farmhouse and spurning two footpath signs on your right (the first of which is waymarked 'Dales Way'). 100 yards past the farm you come upon what appears to be an open air museum of agricultural machinery! You will also see a gate on your left marked Hagg End. Go through and along the cart track to a desolate old farm, the final resting place of several old Austin minis. Walk boldly into the farmyard (staunchly ignoring any barking dogs) and between the house and barn to go through a gateway and into a field.

The footpath now vanishes. Hitherto the landscape has been littered with Dales Way arrows and LDSPB signs – now just when you need them most they fail you. Follow the wire fence on your left, past the old orchard, and you come to a broken stone wall. Cross the wall and continue along it. Past a beck the wall meets an intact stone wall at the top of the field. Look very carefully and you will see a traditional stone stile blending unobtrusively with its surroundings. Climb over and follow a reasonably clear path across the open fellside in front of you. The path climbs the rise, bearing right a little, to give a good view of School Knott with the Langdales and Coniston Old Man beyond. Go downhill towards School Knott (watch out for thistles!), following the line of a broken wall on your right. Arrive at a beck running across the path, cross and follow it right until you come to a small tarn.

Start to skirt the northern (left) edge of the tarn and about half-way round stop and look left. The path is not obvious but you'll see a stone wall, and a wooden stile. Go over the stile and up the next field, bearing slightly left, until you top the brow of the hill to a superb view of the northern stretch of Windermere.

Walk down the field, heading as if towards the town. The path is not too clear, but aim to the right of the trees in the field beyond. You will meet a stone wall and a ladder stile, at the junction of the two stone walls. Cross and follow the wall on your right. It takes you down to a tarmac bridleway behind the houses. Follow this left for about 400 yards, passing a very pretty white cottage on your left and a public footpath sign on your right. The track leads back to Lickbarrow Road. Go left and, after half-a-mile, you come back to Matson Ground. Go through the kissing-gate and retrace your steps across to field to the drive. Through the kissing-gate and into the next field, but this time, instead of bearing left to retrace your earlier route, go straight across the field to a five-bar gate and a white-marked stile in a wall. Cross the next field, go through another stile and as you approach the next stone wall look out for a large boulder ahead of you. This is marked "P.F." with an arrow pointing right. Go right to a tiny little gate in the wall and follow the line of the fence across the next field to Helm Farm.

Go through a gate *and* a stile to come out beside the farm. This is an attractive old farmhouse, built in 1691. Notice the spinning gallery above the door. Continue around the farmhouse and bear left along the lane, past the front of the house. Past Helm Lodge and on to the public road. Go downhill to a junction in the roads, just past Deloraine on your right, and turn left, through a kissing-gate and into the trees, marked 'National Trust – Post Knott. (This is a good area for jays and red squirrels.)

Walk along the track until you come to the crossroads of footpaths again. Turn right and back down Brantfell Road. If you've timed it right, the Hole Int' Wall should just be opening!

WALK 20
PUBS
ENNERDALE

(Bowness Knott – Ben Gill – Anglers Crag)

MAPS:	O/S 1:25,000 Outdoor Leisure Series, 'The English Lakes' , N-W sheet (NB: the whole of this walk is only shown on the most modern, metric sheets).
DISTANCE:	5 3/4 miles (plus 1 mile if detouring to Ennerdale Bridge).
ROUGH GUIDE TO TIME TAKEN:	2 hours.
TERRAIN:	Level and easy for the most part, along well-defined footpaths and country lanes.
FOOD AND DRINK:	Fox and Hounds, Ennerdale Bridge.
TRANSPORT:	Forestry Commission car park at Bowness Knott.
START AND FINISH:	Bowness Knott (Grid reference: 109154).

Ennerdale is the only one of the sixteen lakes which lacks a public road running along its length. Cars are permitted as far as Bowness Knott, thereafter the valley is the exclusive preserve of the walker. The valley bottom is completely given over to Forestry Commission plantations, mainly Norway and sitka spruce with some larch,

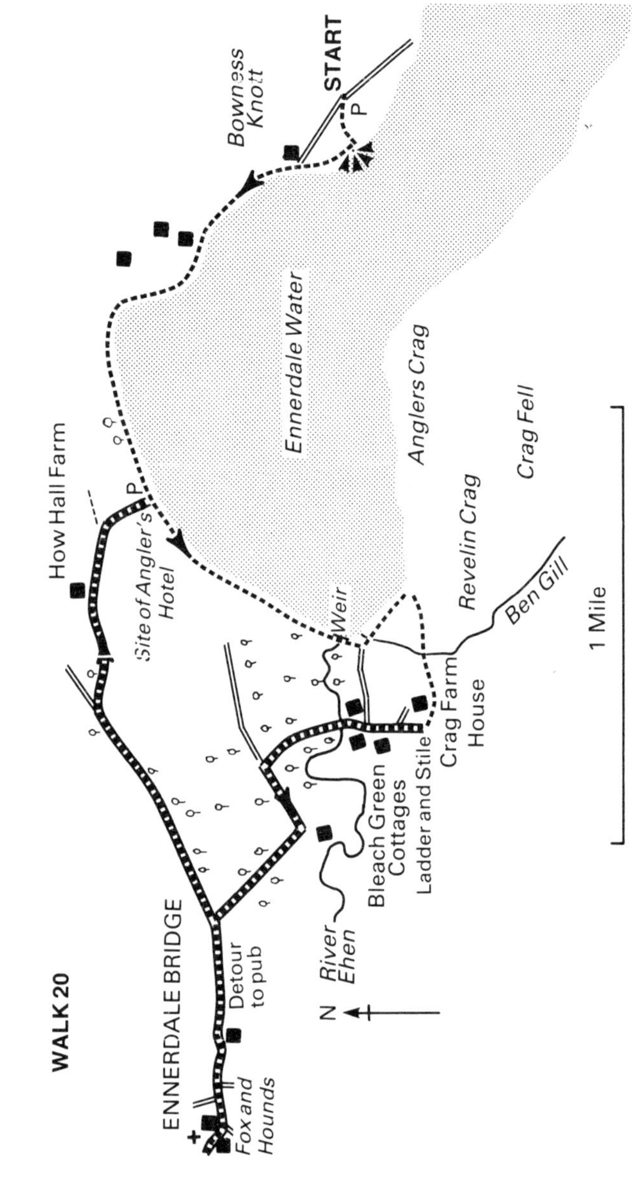
WALK 20
START
Bowness Knott
P
Ennerdale Water
Anglers Crag
Crag Fell
How Hall Farm
P
Site of Angler's Hotel
Revelin Crag
Ben Gill
Weir
1 Mile
Crag Farm House
Ladder and Stile
Bleach Green Cottages
River Ehen
ENNERDALE BRIDGE
Detour to pub
Fox and Hounds
N

Scots pine and sycamore. Initial planting in the 1930's provoked an uproar which later led the Commission to soften the regimented plantations by following the contours of the valley more sympathetically.

The commission's car park at Bowness Knott is the starting point for a number of waymarked trails through the forest, but we will be striking out on our own along the foot of the lake.

Begin by climbing Bowness Knott for a dramatic view of Crag Fell – the near vertical stone wall ascending it is a masterpiece of the waller's art. Walk down to the lakeshore, past what must be among the best-sited picnic tables in the Lake District. Follow the shoreline right to pick up a well-made track which continues along the shore. You pass through several gates, walking beside farmland along a level track with stone banking on the shoreline. The lake itself is a reservoir, owned by the North West Water Authority. The level has been raised to provide water for West Cumbria. No boating is allowed and the water is pure and largely free of nutrients, so there are few fish species present.

The path brings you, after nearly a mile, to another car park. This was once the site of a famous inn, the Angler's Hotel. It was demolished in anticipation of a further rise in the level of the lake (prevented by local protest and vigorous campaigning by bodies such as Friends of the Lake and the National Park Authority). The site is now owned by the National Trust and makes a fine viewpoint (a good alternative starting point for the walk although your car needs good suspension to cope with the rough track down to the park). This point has superb views up to the head of Ennerdale and some of the most spectacular scenery in the Lakes. Above the dark conifers rise the heads of Steeple and Pillar, the latter much favoured by rock climbers. The dale head contains the Lake District's remotest youth hostel, Black Sail. Inaccessible by road, it is reached from the central lakes via Great Gable.

Continue along the track, walking alongside a pleasant broadleaf woodland. In front of you is Ben Gill whilst to the left is Anglers Crag. This dramatic promontory stands at the junction of the Borrowdale volcanic rocks and the Skiddaw slates and is unstable (in geological terms). Eventually it will slide into the lake. The head of the valley contains some of the richest rock architecture in the Lake District. At the end of the track, go through a kissing-gate and on to a grassy path beside fields. Continue through a strange iron 5-bar gate (it has teeth on the top!) and keep left at the fork, running parallel to the shore. The path winds through the gorse bushes across open heath to bear left of the trees. The path then skirts to the right of the NWWA building and arrives at a gate. Go through the kissing-gate alongside and over the bridge.

Ben Gill in front of you now presents a dramatic picture as it tumbles down the face of Revelin Crag. The weir on the left forms the dam. Notice the old square buildings on your right as you cross the bridge. Once over, go left, along the lakeshore. You will come to a tiny footbridge beside a spring. Continue along the shore until you reach a kissing-gate (signed 'N.T. – Anglers Crag'). Go through and right, following the stone wall uphill. The route is easy to follow, although it becomes rough underfoot. It climbs alongside a new forestry plantation to the Gill. Be very careful crossing the wet stepping stones. Cross the fence via the small stile and keep straight on, following your friendly wall.

The path goes through an iron gate and starts to approach Crag Farm House (large and yellow, at the time of writing). Ignore the stile in the fence on your left and carry on past the house, over a stile and then straight on to an elaborate ladder stile in the wall on your right (it's really part-stile and part-ladder). Descend to the field and follow the wire fence to the track which leads to Crag Farm. Turn left along the track and cross a cattle grid next to a pretty little cottage to come on to the tarmac lane next to Bleach Green Cottages. Turn left along the road, over the bridge. Don't be waylaid by invitations into the Forestry Commission picnic area on your right, but continue along the road, through rather nice old woods.

Keep to the road and after $\frac{3}{4}$ mile you will come to a T-junction. To detour to the Fox & Hounds, turn left for $\frac{1}{2}$ mile and the road brings you to Ennerdale Bridge. Keep left at the crossroads, then right at the sign. This a nice old pub, rarely busy, which stands beside the church. To continue walk, retrace your steps to the first road junction. . . If saving the pub until later, turn right at the T-junction and continue along this quiet country lane for perhaps $\frac{2}{3}$ mile until you come to a turning on your right for How Hall Farm (signed: 'N.T. – Ennerdale'). Follow the track, past the farmhouse until you come to Old Anglers Hotel car park and the lakeshore again. Turn left and retrace your steps to Bowness Knott.